William J. Fay

THE BIBLE IN THE CHURCHES

How Various Christians Interpret the Scriptures

KENNETH HAGEN, EDITOR

Second Edition
Marquette University Press
Milwaukee Wisconsin
1994

MARQUETTE STUDIES IN THEOLOGY
4

ANDREW TALLON, SERIES EDITOR

ASSISTANT TO THE EDITOR
ALDEMAR HAGEN

COVER BY WILLIAM HANNAN

PRINTED IN THE UNITED STATES OF AMERICA
ISBN 0-87462-628-5

TABLE OF CONTENTS

PREFACE

First Edition

The idea for this volume on biblical interpretation in the churches grew out of an institute convened by Kenneth Hagen and held at Marquette University in Milwaukee in the summer of 1982. The goal of the project was the exploration of the much acclaimed "crisis" in biblical study. The institute examined the ecumenical significance of biblical study today and in history as a source of both unity and division among the churches.

Kenneth Hagen (Lutheran), professor of theology at Marquette, begins by tracing the history of biblical interpretation from early Christianity to the nineteenth century. The other three contributors assess how the Bible is interpreted in their respective traditions, give an exegesis of a common text (Eph. 2:1-10), and provide some bibliographic suggestions. Although the basic format of these three contributions is the same, the authors were free to discuss whatever they considered most pertinent and most valuable in advancing the conversation.

Daniel J. Harrington, S.J. (Catholic), professor of New Testament at Weston School of Theology in Cambridge, Mass., investigates the extent to which Catholic biblical scholars have accepted and adapted the critical methods developed largely in Protestant circles. Grant R. Osborne (Evangelical), professor of New Testament at Trinity-Evangelical Divinity School in Deerfield, Ill., explains how the evangelical approach to Scripture developed out of the history of the Church in general and out of late nineteenth and early twentieth century American fundamentalism in particular. Joseph A. Burgess (Lutheran), executive director of the Division of Theological Studies for the Lutheran Council/USA in New York, N.Y., deals with some of the underlying theological issues from a Lutheran perspective. The brief conclusion by Harrington tries to focus the areas of convergence and divergence.

Kenneth Hagen organized the 1982 institute, directed the progress of the writing project, and served as general editor of the volume. Daniel J. Harrington acted as copyeditor and worked on relations with the publisher.

Kenneth Hagen
March 1984

PREFACE

Second Edition

In 1985 *The Bible in the Churches* (Paulist), which essentially was a text dedicated to how Catholic, Lutheran, and Evangelical churches have understood and used the Bible, was published. A history of the interpretation of the Bible from the early church to the nineteenth century was also included. The volume sold out by February 1992.

Since the unavailability of *The Bible in the Churches*, I have accepted the challenge to see what could be done to broaden the appeal of a revised volume for college and seminary use. A single volume serves a real need for those interested in how the churches actually apply the Scriptures. No one volume currently exists in English—one that engages the student with the reception of the Scriptures in the major Christian traditions written by representatives of the living traditions.

Included in the revised edition are representatives of the Roman Catholic, Eastern Orthodox, Lutheran, and Evangelical traditions on the history of the Bible in their churches plus a concluding chapter by George Tavard. In an effort to move beyond another volume on the history of hermeneutics, each of the contributors exegetes Ephesians 2:1-10, which gives a concrete example of how the churches read the same text so differently.

Interest in the history of biblical interpretation continues to increase in scholarly historical circles; plus we continue to hear challenges to the contemporary historical-critical methodologies. It is amazing and gratifying that interest in church history as the history of biblical exegesis (Gerhard Ebeling) is actually being done throughout Europe and the United States.

Marquette University Press, Andrew Tallon, Director, became a strong support to press on with a new and revised edition. Aldemar Hagen did the hard technical work.

Kenneth Hagen
December 10, 1993

THE HISTORY OF SCRIPTURE IN THE CHURCH
by
Kenneth Hagen

PART ONE: THE MEDIEVAL CHURCH

Modern biblical scholars have dealt with Scripture since the sixteenth century in terms of the various critical methods. It was not always
that way. The concern for "method," whether in theology or medicine
or logic, etc., became important in the sixteenth century and has continued to dominate the intellectual scene. The crisis today in scriptural
study is due largely to the development of the "historical-critical method"
after the sixteenth century. Since that method has so dominated Protestant approaches to Scripture for centuries and Catholic approaches
more recently, Part Two will look at the rise of the historical-critical
method.

To look at the history of Scripture before the modern church, the
material in Part One will be divided into four sections: (I) The Early
Church, (II) The High Middle Ages, (III) The Late Medieval Period,
and (IV) The Early Reformation. In each case the subdivisions will
treat the place of the Bible in theology, the interpretation of the Bible,
and a key figure (Augustine, Aquinas, Erasmus, and Luther, respec-
tively).

I. THE EARLY CHURCH

A. The Place of the Bible in Theology.

For about the first thousand years theology was *sacra pagina* (sacred page). From the age of the Fathers up to the rise of the schools
(Scholasticism), the source of theology was the sacred page of Scripture. Theology was all wrapped up in the study of God's sacred imprint
in Holy Writ.

Think of the monastery. It was the monastery that preserved learning up to the time of the schools or universities. The monk was the
bearer of classical and Christian civilization. Think of the monk work-

ing with Scripture before the movable printing press and the photo-copier. Think of the disciplined monk copying Scripture, singing it in the holy office, praying it, carrying it in his heart the whole day. The monk lived in the world of the Bible. His whole life was connected with Scripture. It was sometime in the Renaissance (different times for different places) that people began to see a difference between their contemporary culture and the age of the Bible. The monk could not disassociate himself from Scripture. It is hard for us to imagine that because we have the Bible in a black book, we can take it off the shelf and read and then put the book back (out of sight, out of mind). The monk could not put the Bible away. There was no book. The Bible was in his heart.

From the earliest times on, the place of the Bible in theology was that the Bible was theology and theology was the Bible. The Fathers refuted heresies, the monks preserved the Scriptures and Traditions, all on the basis of the Bible. Theology was not some separate discipline as it became in the high Middle Ages and as it is today. For the early period the Bible was the source of all that is—God's work in his creation and in his Church, and that work is encapsulated in the monastery.

B. The Interpretation of the Bible.

The Bible was seen to contain various senses or levels of meaning, sometimes many levels. The Bible was so rich, so full of meaning, that its depth of meaning could not be exhausted by a literal reading. The early church on up to the discovery of Aristotle was influenced by Platonic philosophy. In Platonic philosophy the particular thing (in Scripture, the letter of the text) is a mirror of reality. The reality is the fuller meaning. As the monk reads Scripture he finds shades of meaning far beyond what first meets the eye.

"The letter kills, but the Spirit gives life" (2 Cor 3:6) was New Testament warrant for the Fathers and the monks to distinguish between the literal and the spiritual meaning. The New Testament itself, in its interpretation of the Old, distinguishes between the literal and spiritual meaning. The pattern for interpreting Scripture is contained within Scripture. Interpreting Scripture meant explicating the spiritual depths of meaning. For us, interpretation means bridging the gap between an ancient text and the modern world. When there is only one world, there is no separation. So interpretation meant commenting, annotating, explaining the various levels of meaning the Spirit leads one to see.

The most famous of the multilevel approach became the *quadriga*, the fourfold sense: the literal tells what happened (historical sense), the allegorical teaches what is to be believed, the tropological or moral what is to be done, and the anagogical where it is going or "tending." The usual example is Jerusalem, which refers literally to the city, allegorically to the Church, tropologically to the soul, and anagogically to heaven. The monks put this to rhyme. The point is that the letter of Scripture is a mirror of the almost limitless depth of meaning.

C. The Key Figure Here is St. Augustine.

Augustine pulls together the various strands of patristic exegesis and is the pillar on which the medieval period is built, thus the most important theologian for the entire (thousand year plus) medieval period and on into the sixteenth century. Let us look at how Augustine puts Scripture together, his understanding of Scripture.

Augustine, as is typical throughout this period, sees two eras of salvation represented by the two books of Scripture. The Old Testament and the New Testament represent the old era of salvation and the new era of salvation. The point is that God has a plan for his people, for his creation; and he gives revelation progressively as the people are prepared and able to accept what it is that God has in mind. So there is a progressive revelation going on in Scripture. The ages of Scripture correspond to a person growing up; corporately it is the human race growing up. In the Old Testament the human race is in its infancy or in adolescence, and only as the human race (Israel) became more mature was it ready to receive Christ and the higher revelation. By implication then the fuller understanding of revelation continues in the Church.

Another term that Augustine uses is that God is the "doctor of medicine" and is healing his people. That is what salvation is: health (well-being). That is the goal of this creation, revelation, and finally salvation: final healing. So God the doctor prescribes medicine to the extent that the people will respond and grow until the coming of Christ, who is both the physician and the medicine. Christ is the cure as well as the curer. And that continues on through the life of the Church. So as Augustine looks at Scripture, he sees God's plan, God's providence. He sees two eras of this plan, and in these two eras God is the doctor healing his people.

Augustine also deals with the Scriptures as books. As a theologian he has the Jewish and Christian manuscripts or books to integrate. A great deal of early hermeneutical effort was spent on the relationship between the two great Testaments. Very generally, the New was considered to be the fulfillment of the Old. Augustine emphasized that what was hidden or veiled in the Old Testament was revealed or uncovered in the New Testament. What was prefigured in the Old was made clear in the New. This is a "both . . . and" relationship, thus the necessity of both Testaments: the New is concealed in the Old, and the Old is made clear in the New. Since the Holy Spirit is the author of both, there is unity and harmony between them. The unity of the Testaments and the progress of revelation is the basis of holding that the New Testament is superior to the Old Testament. The New is new in relation to the Old, and vice-versa. Both are needed. The New is more excellent.

So Augustine looks at the Bible in terms of salvation-medicine and healing. He looks at the Bible as a theologian and sees a unity geared towards the superiority of the New Testament as the fulfillment of the Jewish Scriptures. Thirdly, when Augustine looks at Scripture, he sees the two Testaments as two ways of salvation; he sees the two Testaments as two types of people. This is another level on which he looks at Scripture and sees that there is not only the chronological development of the whole race and the whole doctrine, but that there is also the situation that some people of faith back in the Old Testament were actually living ahead of themselves. They were living in the New Testament because they believed Christian doctrine. And he says that in New Testament times there were people who had not seen the message and were still living in the Old Testament because they were living according to the flesh and not according to the Spirit. This is again Augustine's famous letter/Spirit dichotomy, and it becomes an important hermeneutical tool throughout the medieval period on up into modern times. You live according to the letter, or you live according to the Spirit. "The letter kills, the Spirit gives life." So if you live according to the letter, according to the desires of the flesh, you are Old Testament. It does not matter when you live, chronologically speaking, but soteriologically speaking you are old, Augustine says. Or, if you live according to the Spirit and you see the Spirit in the letter of Scripture and can see through the veil to the pure light of Christ and Christian doctrine, then you belong to the New Testament and you are new, no matter whether you are Abraham or someone in the New Testament or someone today. So, on balance, what we have from Augustine is a fairly complicated view of Scripture, a multinuanced view of Scripture; and it is these various strands of putting Scripture together and interpreting Scripture that continue through the medieval period.

In between the early period and the high Middle Ages is something of a transitional period focused on the abbey of Saint Victor in Paris, namely the Victorines. In going from Augustine to Thomas Aquinas via these Victorines, we see that something of hermeneutical shift is underway, a shift that is purported to be developed in Thomas. The important thing about the Victorines is that some of them were oriented towards the literal sense of Scripture, toward the historical sense, and used Jewish exegesis for the understanding of the Old Testament. What we had in the Victorines was not so much a theoretical change; that is, they were really not developing a new hermeneutic as such. But what we got from the Victorines was simply a preoccupation with the literal-historical sense apart from the allegorical or spiritualizing senses.

II. THE HIGH MIDDLE AGES

A. The Place of the Bible in Theology.

Here it is important to think of the school, the university. This period becomes known as Scholasticism because theology is connected to the schools. The schools are the newly founded universities. Theology and the study of Scripture underwent quite a shift as they moved from the monastery to the university classroom. We have pictured the monk living, praying, eating, and sleeping Scripture, living his life in the context of the life of Scripture; whereas in the school, not unlike our present situation, Scripture is a subject of academic study. What we get in the school approach is a distinction or separation between theology and exegesis, a distinction or separation between the discipline of theology and the discipline of biblical interpretation. This is in part because of the influence of Aristotelian philosophy away from Platonic philosophy. With Aristotle, reality is seen contained in the thing itself. Hence in scriptural study, attention shifts to the sense of the letter. With the reality seen in the thing itself, rather than being mirrored into some other-worldly realm of the spiritual, Scripture itself becomes the object of study. What the Holy Spirit intended to say is there in Scripture, and all the levels of meaning are in the letter of the text, not in some other levels of meaning.

With a shift in scriptural study there is a shift in theology. While work on the Bible becomes more "literal" and "historical" (though, remember, we are still in the twelfth and thirteenth centuries), theology becomes speculative. An important influence on this shift in theology is the interest in dialectic (a part of logic). In the university situation, dialectic is the analysis of a question. Speculation is looking into something. It could and did have mystical overtones because theology first and foremost is looking into God. A question is posed, alternatives analyzed, often followed by a resolution. The shift in theology is a shift away from *sacra pagina* to *sacra doctrina* (sacred doctrine). The first question in Thomas' *Summa theologiae* is: What is sacred doctrine? Work on the sacred page is contained in the *Commentaries* on Scripture. Theological questions are dealt with in the *Summaries* of Theology (there were summaries in other disciplines as well). Theology then has a life of its own. Scripture and the Fathers are the authorities (footnotes). The method is philosophical, faith seeking understanding.

B. The Interpretation of the Bible.

Accompanying the separation of Bible and theology is a different approach to the Bible (with Aristotle and reason in the background). For a Platonist, the soul (spirit) was seen hidden or imprisoned in the body (letter). The Aristotelian sees the spirit expressed by the text. All meaning is expressed in the letter, authored by God. The focus shifts away from the mirror of universal truths to the intention of the author (letter). To understand the author is to discern the words and their significance. The Latin word to understand (*intelligere*) means to read within, to penetrate the rational meaning. The truth of the matter is there in the Bible expressed by the letters.

So far in Scholasticism we have the separation of biblical study from the study of theology, a different approach to theology (*sacra doctrina*), and a different approach to Scripture (intention of the letter). Also we have something of a new hermeneutic; at least a great deal is made of that in the literature. (One is always suspicious of new theories, because in the practice of biblical interpretation, the traditional results usually pertain.) This new theory is seen developed by the important fourteenth-century Franciscan biblical scholar, Nicholas of Lyra, who in turn was the most important biblical commentator for the later

Middle Ages and early Reformation. The new hermeneutic is called the "double-literal sense": two senses or meanings expressed by the one letter or word. There is the historical-literal sense and the spiritual- or prophetic-literal sense. The example given is that Solomon may refer to Solomon the man or be a figure of Christ or both. If both, both were intended by the author, the Holy Spirit. As will be seen with Thomas, grounding everything in the letter does not preclude the use of the traditional fourfold sense (literal, allegorical, tropological, and anagogical). The theory of the double-literal sense is widely accepted in the later Middle Ages (via Thomas and Nicholas). The result is an increasing attention to the text.

C. The Key Figure in the High Middle Ages is Thomas Aquinas.
In the modern period Thomas is famous for his *Summa theologiae* (Summary of Theology). In the century following his own, his commentaries on Scripture were more influential. Note that the Aristotelian Thomas wrote on Scripture, and in a separate literary genre he wrote on theology. As an Aristotelian thinks in terms of causality rather than reflection, Thomas thinks of God as the first author of Scripture and the human authors as instruments of divine revelation, choosing their own words. The letter contains the intention of the inspired writer. Thomas outlined his approach to biblical interpretation in the following statement:

> The author of Holy Scripture is God, in whose power it is to signify his meaning, not by words only (as man also can do) but by things themselves. So, whereas in every other science things are signified by words, this science has the property that the things signified by the words have themselves also a signification. Therefore that first signification whereby words signify things belongs to the first sense, the historical or literal. That signification whereby things signified by words have themselves also a signification is called the spiritual sense, which is based on the literal, and presupposes it. For as the apostle says (Heb 10:1) the Old Law is a figure of the New Law, and (Pseudo-) Dionysius says: 'The New Law itself is a figure of future glory.' Again, in the New Law, whatever our Head had done is a type of what we ought to do. Therefore, so far as the things of the Old Law signify the things of the New Law, there is the allegorical sense; so far as the things done in Christ or so far as the things which signify Christ are types of what we ought to do, there is the moral sense. But so far as they signify what relates to eternal glory, there is the anagogical sense. Since the literal sense is that which the author intends, and since the author of Holy Scripture is God, it is not unfitting, as Augustine says, if

even according to the literal sense one word in Holy Scripture should
have several senses.[1]

Thomas presents a relationship between the Old and New Testaments along the lines of sign and fulfillment. The pattern is from Old
to New to "future glory." Augustine is cited to show that in one literal
sense there are several (spiritual) meanings. (It is always amazing how
current Augustine is for the medievals on into the sixteenth century.)
God is at work in the Old through types and signs of the New. In
seeing the signs one sees the relationship between Old and New, and in
seeing the spiritual sense of the New one sees the relationship between
the New Testament and the Church. In the allegorical, moral, and
anagogical senses, God uses visible words to signify invisible truths.
The pattern of relationship, fulfillment, development from Old to New
to Church is the pattern of Thomas' theology, and his interpretation
of Scripture fits within that organic pattern.

For Thomas, there is an organic unity between Old and New.
Augustine's view of the progress of revelation is expanded by Thomas
to include everything from beginning to end, from creation to history,
through the history of Israel, Old and New, to the end of time. Thomas' view of revelation is that it is salvation history developing
organically. God is working salvation in history, and so the history of
God's people is salvation history. The history of salvation in Scripture
is the development from Old to New, old law to evangelical law. The
unity is based on God. The organic continuum goes on in the Church
to "eternal glory."

The main focus of Thomas on the Old and New Testament is on
their organic development, a part of the larger focus of salvation history. In terms of Augustine's approach and categories, Thomas'
approach is a blend of the providential and hermeneutical foci. The
blend is seeing Testament as both era and book. Certain things concerning Christ are prefigured in the Old Testament through figures
like David and Solomon. This is so because things of Christ are of such
magnitude and power that they could not have been introduced "sud-
denly": "The things of Christ are so great that they would not have
been believed unless they had first been disseminated gradually through

---

[1]   Aquinas, *Summa theologiae* I.1.10.

the growth of time."[2] The development in time (era of salvation) is the development from imperfect to perfect. Also the Old Testament is a "figure" of the New Testament. The New Testament church is a "figure" of the glory of heaven. With the development of "figure," Old to New and New to glory, the Old Testament is a "figure of the figure." The development is the development of clarity. Thomas also refers the relationship of Old and New Law to the relationship of seed to tree, implicit to explicit, fear to love. The growth is continual.

III. THE LATE MEDIEVAL PERIOD

A. and B. Scripture and Theology.

The fourteenth and fifteenth centuries are a mixture of what went before and some new currents of thought and practice. The schools continue to be the main focus of theological and biblical studies. There are currents of spirituality (for example, German mysticism and *Devotio moderna*) where the approach to Scripture is more along the monastic lines of *sacra pagina*. Among the Nominalists (a new philosophy-theology) and others, attention is paid to the relation of the Scriptures to the Traditions of the Church. Tension and even conflict between them is posited. The concentration on Scripture as an ancient book and the use of Scripture to criticize the Church is intensified in the (very) late medieval movement of Humanism.

The fourfold method continues. The double-literal sense is used. The imitation of Christ is another emphasis. The use of Jewish resources for a more historical understanding of the Old Testament increases. Study of Hebrew and Greek grows tremendously. All of these interests and approaches are filtered into the Reformation through the Humanists. The most important work on Scripture at the beginning of the sixteenth century was done by the Humanists. In the Catholic Reformation the Humanists lead the way for critical editions of Scripture, vernacular translations, and the study of the Greek and Latin classics (as opposed to the Scholastics). They were defeated at the mid-sixteenth century Council of Trent. It has been in our century that Catholics

---

[2]   Cited in K. Hagen, *A Theology of Testament in the Young Luther* (Leiden: Brill, 1974) 47.

have adopted Humanist and modern critical approaches to Scripture. The Protestants generally welcomed and used Humanist scholarship.

The Humanists were involved in all kinds of humane studies. For our purposes let us peg their efforts around the printing press and the production of sacred literature (*sacra littera*). So the approaches to Scripture in the medieval church differed as it was handled by the monks (*sacra pagina*), by the schoolmen (*sacra doctrina*), and by the printers (*sacra littera*). That is an enormous development, the effects of which we are still appropriating: the relation of the Holy Book to the traditions of the Church, to the study of theology, and to the life of faith.

The effect of the Humanists on the place and interpretation of Scripture in the Church centered around their sense of history, study of the classics, expertise in the biblical (original) languages, preparation of critical printed editions of the Bible, and the use of Scripture for the reform of the Church. (Note that their effect on the place and interpretation of Scripture is on the Church in general, not just on theology, since their programs were broader than technical theology.)

A growing sense among the Renaissance thinkers (south of the Alps) and Humanists (north) was that the historical past is distant and different from present culture. This sense was not universally accepted, and it took until about the nineteenth century for historical consciousness to be widely accepted and then largely only in Western culture. Their sense of history was that the time and place of classical culture was in the ancient world—not their own. In general for the medievals the age of the Bible was their own, a timelessness to it all. The Humanists perspective was the separation of past from present.

The Humanists were scholars, students of antiquity. The general Renaissance of the time was a revival of the arts, literature, and learning. The Humanists were interested in the learning contained in classical literature. The study of the classics was to go along with the study of Scripture, which also was from the classical world, for the purpose of moral and intellectual reform of the Church, theology, philosophy, education—the whole program. The critical study of the past had the edge to it of informing and often attacking the present. The study of the past included the editing, printing, and learning from the church fathers.

The Humanists were part and parcel of the revival of Hebrew and Greek studies. Study of the ancient world meant the recovery of their languages. Study of the original languages of Scripture raised questions about the Latin Bible. The study of the Bible in the original often lead to a criticism of the way the Bible had been translated into Latin and interpreted. Study of ancient languages was not what we would call strictly an academic exercise. Ancient literature—classical and Christian—was presumed to have value. The Humanists were often critical of Scholastics and others who concentrated only on the literal meaning of the text.

Humanist interest in original languages included an interest in original manuscripts and codices. With their historical perspective on the editing, translating, and transmission of texts, they were concerned to get as far back as possible to the original version of a writing. For scriptural study, this concern led to the discovery, collating, and printing of early Hebrew and Greek codices of the Bible. In 1516 Erasmus published the first Greek New Testament. The sixteenth century witnessed several critical editions of the Bible, printed by movable type. The new method in printing made possible the multiplication of both critical editions and vernacular translations.

The study of the classics, the Bible, and church fathers was critical and scholarly. The purpose of it was to reform the present. The Humanists were among those who were disturbed about corruption, lack of education, and the generally sorry state of society. The Church was often blamed for most of it, blamed for being too interested in money, politics, war, everything but the care of souls. The attacks were bitter and sarcastic. Theology (Scholasticism) was reproached for being interested only in syllogisms and not the simple piety of Scripture. The goal of their work was the reform of Church and society through education for the purpose of piety and knowledge.

C. The Key Figure among the Humanists was Erasmus of Rotterdam.

Writing at the turn of the sixteenth century (died in 1536), Erasmus was very critical. He lambasted the superstitions of current monastic practice, the ritualism and legalism connected with the Mass, Scholastic theology (especially its preoccupation with propositions, corollaries, definitions and conclusions), the worldliness of the Pope (especially his preoccupation with war, money, excommunications and interdicts), the begging of mendicant friars, clerical concubinage, and so on. The basis of his attacks was a call to return to the source of Scripture in its purity and original meaning for Christian living. The "pagan" classics and church fathers were to serve as an orientation to Scripture.

Erasmus edited and published a number of the works of the Fathers. Against criticism, he continued to advocate the study of the classics. "A sensible reading of the pagan poets and philosophers is a good preparation for the Christian life." He distinguishes between the bad morals of the pagans, which are not to be followed, and their many examples of right living. "To break in on" Scripture without the preparation of the classics is "almost sacrilegious." "St. Cyprian has worked wonders in adorning the Scriptures with the literary beauty of the ancients."[3] So guided by the Fathers of the Church, classical studies were taken as a necessary introduction to understanding Christian revelation.

Schooled by the Brethren of the Common Life (a part of late medieval *Devotio moderna*), Erasmus' orientation to theology was away from speculation toward piety. His orientation to Scripture, the source of Christian piety, was toward the example of Jesus. The ethical life, preaching, and teaching of Jesus combine into the philosophy of Christ, the source of reform for everything from the papacy to peasantry.

Erasmus' main interest and work was on the New Testament. His Greek New Testament with critical annotations was a milestone in Reformation work on the Bible. It was used by Luther immediately. Erasmus could be very critical of the people of the Old Testament, for their superstitious and barbarous ways, in comparison with the "good letters" from Greece and Rome. In medieval terms his approach to the New Testament was largely tropological—as in Christ, so in me.

Erasmus' sarcasm against Scholastic theology included his charge of supercilious speculation, especially their use of dialectic. Theology was too intellectually preoccupied with doctrine, and not with its main task—persuading and bringing people to the way of Christ. Practical piety is the point of it all. When contemporary commentators dealt with the New Testament, Erasmus complained that they concentrated only on the literal sense:

> Let me mention another requirement for a better understanding of Holy Scripture [the first being reading Scripture with a clean heart]. I would suggest that you read those commentators who do not stick so closely to the literal sense. The ones I would recommend most

---

[3]   *Enchiridion* (1503) cited in *The Essential Erasmus*, J.P. Dolan, ed. (New York: New American Library, 1964) 36.

highly after St. Paul himself are Origen, Ambrose, Jerome, and Augustine. Too many of our modern theologians are prone to a literal interpretation, which they subtly misconstrue. They do not delve into the mysteries, and they act as if St. Paul were not speaking the truth when he says that our law is spiritual. There are some of these theologians who are so completely taken up with these human commentators that they relegate what the Fathers had to say to the realm of dreams. They are so entranced with the writings of Duns Scotus that, without ever having read the Scriptures, they believe themselves to be competent theologians. I care not how subtle their distinctions are; they are certainly not the final word on what pertains to the Holy Spirit.[4]

In their theology the Scholastics were too speculative; in their commentaries on Scripture they were too literal. So a leading scholar of the Renaissance calls for a pious reading of the Bible as the source for Christian living.

IV. THE EARLY REFORMATION

A. The Place of the Bible in Theology.

The early Reformers, for example, Luther, Zwingli, Calvin, were very concerned about the place of Bible in everything— Church, theology, and especially preaching. The main point of the Reformation was that the Gospel must be proclaimed. To keep our schematization going (monastery—university—printing press), now think pulpit, think of the Evangelical cities (Wittenberg, Zurich, Geneva) where the medium for information was the pulpit (along with the important pamphlets). The Reformation was a movement of the Word: Christ, Scripture, preaching—in that order. They all are the Word of God. The Reformers used the printed Word, studied the Word, prayed the Word. But their concern was to bring preaching back into the Mass, preaching in the vernacular, and preaching on the text of Scripture. When Luther said that the Church is not a pen-house but a mouth-house, he meant that the good news cannot properly be put in (dead) letters but is to be proclaimed loudly (in German).

What the Scholastics separated—theology and commentary on Scripture—the early Reformers sought to bring together again, along

---

4   *Ibid.*, 37.

the lines of *sacra pagina* (minus the monastery). Scripture alone is the sole authority for the Church, the discipline of theology, and the life of faith. The Reformers continued the call for the reform of the Church on the basis of Scripture. Every office and activity in the Church falls under the judgment of Scripture. All of theology is contained in Scripture. God has revealed all that we need to know about him in Christ. Calvin is especially strong on the knowledge of God, the beginning point of the *Institutes of the Christian Religion.* God is revealed in Scripture, and to see the revelation of God in nature we need the spectacles of Scripture. Theology must be biblical theology; any other kind is human invention.

Scripture is its own authority because it is clear. No other authority is needed to see through its meaning. The early Reformers were not concerned about some theory of inspiration. That came later. The Bible is the Word. The Reformers were aware of the "critical" discussions among the Humanists about the text, authorship, language, etc. Luther engaged in some of this. The point of the Word is the presence of the Word in Scripture-Church-preaching. The Humanist sense of the distance of Scripture from the present was not accepted. The scholastic separation of theology from Scripture was attacked. The purpose of theology is to serve preaching, the main task of the Church. The vast amount of theological literature from the early Reformation was intended to clear the roadblocks to Scripture and to facilitate the proclamation of that Gospel.

B.   The Interpretation of the Bible.

The early Reformers were premodern; they continued the general medieval understanding of interpretation as commentary, annotation, and exposition. The modern interpreter continues to develop the Humanist perspective of the historical past; thus interpretation in modern time is bridging the gulf between ancient literature and modern thinking. The early Reformers continued the monkish approach of total immersion into the thinking and language of Scripture so that there is only one language, one biblical theology.

In their Catholic context, the Reformers emphasized that Scripture was its own interpreter. Luther argued that the papacy had built a wall of authoritative interpretation around itself so that Scripture could only be read as the papacy interpreted it. One late medieval synthesis had it that Scripture is to Tradition as foundation is to interpretation

(Occam). Strong in the sixteenth century was the question of an authoritative interpretation of Scripture. The Catholic Council of Trent decreed

> that no one, relying on his own skill, in matters of faith, and of morals pertaining to the edification of Christian doctrine, wresting the Sacred Scriptures to his own senses, presume to interpret the said Sacred Scripture contrary to that sense which holy mother church, whose it is to judge of the true sense and interpretation of the Holy Scripture, has held and does hold.[5]

For Calvin at this time, the interpretation of Scripture by Scripture alone is aided by the internal testimony of the Holy Spirit. Scripture itself attests to its message and meaning. Christ and the Spirit are at work in the Word. The Reformers insisted that postapostolic claims of authoritative interpretation were precisely the reason why the Word of God lost its/his central place in the life of the Church.

The Reformation interpretation of Scripture was caught up in theological polemics. The Humanists used Scripture to attack the Church, but they were not so much interested in the pure doctrines of Scripture as they were in exposing the corruption and folly of the present situation in the light of the piety of Scripture. The early Reformers fought for pure doctrine on the basis of Scripture (and the Fathers). The doctrine of justification by faith alone, by grace alone (by Christ alone), was seen as the central doctrine of Scripture. The doctrine of justification by faith is the criterion by which all other doctrines, offices, and practices in the Church are judged. The criteriological priority of justification by faith is established in Scripture. The Church stands or falls, said Luther, on the scriptural teaching of justification. There were other issues, other polemics, but the procedure was the same. Doctrinal reform was forged and pleaded on the basis of Scripture.

C. In the Early Reformation Period Martin Luther was the Key Figure.

Basic for Luther's understanding of Scripture was his distinction between law and Gospel. The Gospel of Jesus Christ is the fulfillment and end of the Mosaic law. Law and Gospel are in all books of the Bible. The Gospel is the good news that salvation is in Christ alone. Abraham and others saw that Gospel in the promises, believed, and

---

[5]   P. Schaff, *The Creeds of Christendom*, Vol. 2 (New York: Harper, 1919) 83.

were justified. Luther transposes Augustine's distinction between Old Testament and New Testament as ways of salvation to law and Gospel as ways of salvation. The way of the law is do this...and don't do that....The way of the Gospel is believe...and it has already been done for you (in Christ). The law is command, the Gospel is gift, the gift of forgiveness. When the law commands, failure results because one cannot fulfill the law on one's own power ("The good I would, I do not"). The law humbles; the Gospel picks up. One cannot be picked up unless one is put down to size. Being brought low (law) and being raised up (Gospel) are the ups and downs of the Christian life, the experience of sin (brought by the law), and the experience of forgiveness (brought by Christ). The distinction between law and Gospel, the doctrine of justification by faith apart from works, and the understanding of the core of Scripture are all the same for Luther.

The center of Scripture for Luther is Christ, present in both the Old Testament and the New Testament. Christ is the eternal Word of God, present in Old Testament times in the form of promise, present in New Testament times in the person of Jesus, and present in the Church through Word and sacrament. In all cases, Christ the Word is the effective means of grace (healing salvation for Augustine). The center or core of Scripture is "what drives Christ" (*was Christum treibet*) (impossible to translate literally), i.e., what preaches Christ, what promotes or points to Christ. Christ is at the core of God's plan of salvation. God promises through prophets; God delivers in person. All of Scripture leads to Christ, and Christ leads to salvation.

Luther's response to the various senses of meaning in the Middle Ages (fourfold, double-literal) was that Scripture has one simple sense (most often, Christ). Or Luther will talk about the grammatical sense as the meaning of the text, that the grammatical meaning and theological meaning are the same. Luther availed himself of Humanist scholarship (and Humanists saw an early ally in Luther) and was a part of a late medieval trend to highlight (once again) the christological meaning of a text. Luther also used allegory, not to establish a doctrine, he said, but to embellish it. He also used the other spiritual senses. Luther on Scripture is often presented as a total break from the medieval world. That came later. (You can take the boy out of the monastery, but you cannot take the monastery out of the boy.) In the area of the senses of meaning, Luther is a part of the medieval trend to call for a return to the letter of the text, and then, in practice, to go on and find other senses of meaning. After all (and all the medievals knew this) the New Testament itself uses allegory.

Luther's distinction is his construction of Scripture as containing a single testament (will, promise) of Christ. God's last and only will and testament is that he would die for our salvation. The promise is the declaration of the will and testament. The death of the God-Man validates his testament. The inheritance is the forgiveness of sins and eternal life. The (new) testament of Christ is eternal. It is played out in time, but there is no development in the eternal. Augustine and the medievals generally saw a development and transformation within and between the Old and New Testament. Luther held that the New Testament is older than the Old because it is the oldest (eternal). The Old Testament begins and ends in time.

We have come a long way (to the sixteenth century). Or have we? What often is seen to be new is not so new after all. The monastery (*sacra pagina*), the university (*sacra doctrina*), the printing press (*sacra littera*), and the pulpit (Holy Gospel) all represent shifts and emphases. The whole enterprise, however, was still "sacred."

PART TWO: THE MODERN CHURCH

In the modern period the historical-critical method dominates most Protestant approaches to Scripture and, since 1943 (*Divino Afflante Spiritu*), also most Catholic approaches. By the middle of the eighteenth century the historical-critical method is in place. One way of picturing the shift that takes place between the medieval approach (including early Reformation) and the modern approach of the later seventeenth and eighteenth century is to consider their views of the relation between the letter and the real, between the text of Scripture and what really happened. In the medieval approach the letter of the Bible was read as historical and real; there was no question that what was said really happened. Scripture was read as religion, history, geography, liturgy, prayer, and so on. The approach of historical criticism is first to question the relation between the letter and the real, then to posit a separation between the two, and finally to see the text as a faith response to a real stimulus. What we have in the text are the responses of the communities of faith, not the stimuli. In the nineteenth century it was said that what we have in the New Testament is the Christ of faith and not the Jesus of history. In any case, it came to be perceived in historical criticism that the Bible is the interpretation of facts and not the bare facts themselves. It was written from faith to (our) faith.

The historical-critical method is concerned about the origin of individual books of the Bible. Concerned about the books as theological literature and not history, it uses the best critical (objective, analytic) tools available for the study of ancient literature. The modern approach develops some of the humanist interests detailed earlier—interest in the historical past, the original text, and language.

There were and are various methods within the historical-critical method. These will be detailed by others in this volume. Here the concern will be to trace the rise of the historical-critical method, to detail the shift from medieval-early Reformation to (early) modern approaches (from the middle of the sixteenth century to late eighteenth century). Generally the medievals treated Scripture as the Church's holy book. The moderns increasingly treat Scripture with secular tools of historical and literary criticism in order to understand it better in its ancient setting.

Among the elements that contributed to the rise of the historical-critical method include the following: (1) methodology (discussion of the way of interpretation), (2) Deism (rational belief in the deity, with resultant rationalism and the disciplines of biblical introduction and biblical theology), (3) textual criticism (analysis of codices, variant readings, with both theory and practice), and (4) historical consciousness (awareness of distance and difference, e.g., seeing the difference between stimulus and response).

1. **Methodology.** Theology became interested in the questions of "method" in the sixteenth century.[6] In 1555 Nils Hemmingsen, a student of Luther and Melanchthon (especially the latter), published a book *On Methods*, the first part for philosophy, the second for theological method. It was important because of its subject—*methodus*. Earlier in the sixteenth century method as a technical term came into medicine, and in the second half of the century lawyers discussed method. So theology joined the other branches of learning in their concern to tidy up their discipline. Also important is that Hemmingsen brought logic (particularly dialectic) into theology in the discussion of method. For biblical study what this meant was that discussion of exegetical method" (the way to interpret) was carried on in the part on philosophical method, and then practiced in theology and "exegesis," the actual word being used.

"Exegesis" is widely used in the seventeenth and eighteenth century as the art for interpreting Scripture. Exegesis is an ancient and early modern word, not to be found in ecclesiastical Latin in the ancient or medieval period. Medieval work on Scripture was done in the genre of commentary and annotation. "Interpretation" meant the translation and explanation of obscure and enigmatic words or dreams. Modern "interpretation" presupposes a historical separation between the interpreter and the text; and in the case of the "methodists," there is the necessity of first discussing the method or way of interpreting before the actual interpretation or exegesis takes place. For Luther, Scripture was its own interpreter. The difference is that the (early) modern becomes conscious of the discipline, or problem, of interpretation.

---

6 K. Hagen, "'De exegetica methodo,' Niels Hemmingsen's De Methodis (1555)," *The Bible in the Sixteenth Century*, David Steinmetz, ed. ("Duke Monographs in Medieval and Renaissance Studeies," Vol. 11; Durham, NC: Duke University Press, 1990) 181-96, 252-55.

What comes out of this work on method of interpretation is reflection on the need for an introduction to a biblical book. Already in the third quarter of the sixteenth century, this is found in Hemmingsen and Matthias Flacius Illyricus who is often credited with being the father of modern hermeneutics. In Hemmingsen's methodology four questions need to be asked in an introduction to a particular book of the Bible in order that it will be understood "more explicitly," "more skillfully and correctly," "more easily," or "more clearly." In the introduction the first question of *authorship* determines the authority of the writing. The second, the *occasion*, leads to an understanding of the literary structures. The third, the *status* or principal question of the writing, leads to a perception of the ultimate goal and scope of the whole writing. The fourth is the *method* or order of presentation. Flacius also reflects on the need for an introduction, covering the same four questions, before one begins with the biblical writing itself.

The shift away from the medieval-early Reformation to early modern approaches, somewhere in the middle of the sixteenth century, is seen in the modern focus on the proper order of methodology, introduction, exegesis, in other words, on the problem of interpretation (hermeneutics). For the medievals there was no problem of interpretation. There were rules for reading Scripture, summarized by Luther as prayer, meditation, and experience. For the modern, these become hindrances rather than helps. The modern needs a method to understand. Luther often said he needed more time.

2.   Deism. To discuss the next major advances in the rise of the historical-critical method would mean jumping to the late seventeenth and eighteenth century, with the developments in Deism and rationalism and in textual criticism. To understand the attacks from these quarters, generically all rationalists, one needs to see what it was they were attacking, namely, what is known within (Western) Europe and Protestantantism as Orthodoxy and Pietism.

In the later sixteenth and seventeenth century the question of method in theology was central in Lutheran and Reformed Orthodoxy. The concern was for pure doctrine in its proper place in the dogmatic system. Scripture is the source for systematic and doctrinal theology. In the give and take with Roman theologians, the Orthodox Protestants developed nuanced theories of the inspiration of Scripture, the only infallible authority. Revealed theology is drawn only from the revealed Word. Scripture is divine, supernatural revelation. It is the very Word of God in its letters, words, doctrines, and precepts. Scripture is the instrumental source of theology: God is the "principle of the being" of theology—the first cause of theology; and Scripture is the "principle of knowing" God—hence the instrument of theology.

Their theory of inspiration is known as the dictation theory. The definition of inspiration was that act of God whereby he conveyed the content of what he wanted to be written and the very words expressing that content. It is also the doctrine of plenary inspiration—everything in Scripture was inspired and dictated. If the inspiration of one verse is denied, the inspiration, authority, and infallibility of the whole Bible falls. It is also the doctrine of verbal inspiration—every word. The Holy Spirit actually dictated the very words. The biblical authors were defined as "secretaries," hands of Christ or penmen of the Holy Spirit. It is also the doctrine of inerrancy—the secretaries were kept from error in the writing by the Holy Spirit. The method of inspiration was discussed in much detail. The effect was to secure a supernatural revelation (Scripture) that was inerrant, authoritative, sufficient, clear, and efficacious.

The responses to Orthodoxy in the late seventeenth and eighteenth century were as different as Pietism is from rationalism. And Orthodoxy did not die. Hence a three-ring circus, which is still being played today.

What is a Pietist? He's one who hears the Word.

And lives a holy life in terms of what he's heard. There were Pietists in seventeenth-century England, Holland, and Germany. They were interested in nontheological study of the Bible for personal experience and holiness. They were more interested in the effect of Scripture than its origin. Scripture was the source of providential guidance for the pious. They encouraged direct access to the Bible without postbiblical interpretation. They were (and are) responsible for the massive distribution of inexpensive editions of the Bible. The developing historical-critical method was of little or no interest. The Pietists were in opposition to the rationalism of the age. A Bible in everyone's hand. For the Orthodox, the Bible was a source book of doctrine; for the Pietist, it was the mirror of holiness.

A rival to Orthodoxy and Pietism, but way over on the secular side of things where the historical-critical method was developing, was

Enlightenment Christianity. Enlightenment Christianity included English Deists, Dutch skeptics, French naturalists, and German rationalists—all generically rationalists.

A central concern of the English Deists and others to follow was to attack supernational views of revelation and to argue rather for natural religion—the natural, the rational, and the universal. Three works, typical and influential, from the Deists were John Locke, *The Reasonableness of Christianity* (1695); John Toland, *Christianity Not Mysterious* (1696); and Matthew Tindal, *Christianity as Old as Creation* (1730). Reason is the judge of revelation. Belief in the Creator God (Deity) is reasonable; but belief in God's subsequent intervention—prophecies, miracles, atonement—is not reasonable and therefore rejected. The truth of Christianity must be discoverable in all ages. Natural religion is the innate core of all religion. The universality of reason is the only criterion of truth. The authority of the biblical record is doubtful.

What comes then from the Deists, naturalists, and rationalists is that the enlightened are freed from the dogmatics of Orthodoxy and any supernatural theory of inspiration. Doctrines like the divinity of Christ, original sin, atonement, sacraments, and miracles are put aside. The New Testament never meant them to be taken seriously. Views of the supernatural were regarded as superstition. Scripture was interpreted historically and critically. The "unworthy," "impossible," and "unreasonable" parts of Scripture were explained away.

By the middle of the eighteenth century (John D. Michaelis, *Introduction to the New Testament*, 1750), the discipline of biblical introduction is in place. We have seen writing about biblical introductions already in the second half of the sixteenth century with Hemmingsen and Flacius. Their reflection on the need for an introduction in order to prepare the way for understanding the book more clearly is not recognized in secondary literature. Richard Simon, a French Catholic in the seventeenth century, is often credited with being the "forerunner" of the discipline of introduction (1678, *Critical History of the Old Testament*; three volumes on the New Testament, 1689-93).

In this discipline the Bible is treated as ancient literature with a historical setting. To understand a writing is to understand its situation in time and space, the book's setting-in-life. An introduction raises all the questions necessary to understand the book. In one introduction, Michaelis asks the following questions: What type of literature is it? Where is it cited elsewhere? To whom is it written? What was its place in the community? When was it written and in what language? What questions are there about the Greek translation? Who wrote it? What about the literary technique? Is it canonical? What is its content? In this line-up there are ten questions raised before the question of content, because the message is linked to its historical place.

The discipline of introduction presupposes the relativity of each book. Each book is unique unto itself and demands a thorough, objective (i.e., critical) study in order to understand it. Later in the eighteenth century, John Eichhorn developed further the humanist-rationalist introduction (three volumes on the Old Testament, 1780-83). The Old Testament must be studied like any other literature, free from all authorities, dogma, and tradition.

The discipline of biblical theology follows closely on the discipline of biblical introduction. The discipline of biblical theology, seen by some as the crown of biblical scholarship, comes out of the Enlightenment and the critical methodologies we have been detailing. More particularly, Gotthold Lessing's *Education of Mankind* (1780) constructed a view of the Bible which parochialized it as preparatory to the maturation of the human race. The Old Testament came at the stage of the childhood of the race, which was motivated by temporal rewards and punishments (law). The New Testament fits into the adolescence of the race, where one is willing to put up with temporary hardships with the promise of greater (spiritual) rewards later (resurrection). And finally the race matured into adulthood by the time of the Enlightenment, where one lives in the here and now guided by reason alone. In effect, then, the Bible is put in its time and place.

Later in the eighteenth century the concern was to separate biblical theology from dogmatic theology (1758, *The Advantage of Biblical Theology over Scholasticism*; 1787, *The Difference between Biblical Theology and Dogmatic Theology*). Dogmatic theology, perhaps connected to philosophy, could have permanence, while biblical theology is connected to its history. Late eighteenth century romanticism, with its emphasis on empathy, aided the discipline of biblical theology. Something like today's nostalgia, one could emotionally immerse oneself into the spirit of a past generation. Biblical theology is the theology of a book. If a book has a human situation—authorship, time, audience, language, purpose, content, method—then it also has a particular theology. As there are various books with various historical situations, so there are various books with various theologies. As a result of this eigh-

teenth-century development, there is no such thing as biblical theology
in the singular, only biblical theologies (plural).

Rationalism, connected with Deism, led to the rise of biblical introduction and theologies, as well as with advances in textual criticism,
all a part of the developing historical-critical method.

3. Textual criticism. Erasmus' text of the Greek New Testament,
the first published in 1516, as mentioned earlier, remained the "critical"
edition (*textus receptus*) until well into the nineteenth century. Although
the Complutensian Polyglot relied on earlier manuscript evidence, and
was actually printed earlier (*New Testament*, 1514) though made public
in 1522, and is now regarded as better, it was Erasmus' text, through
subsequent editions, that was "received by all" (*textus receptus*) and
seemed to have an over three hundred year right to be. Robert Stephanus'
text (Paris, 1550), which followed Erasmus (1535 edition), became the
textus receptus for Britain. The edition of the printing firm, Elzevir
(Leiden, 1633), which followed Stephanus, became the *textus receptus*
for the Continent. Richard Simon, later in the seventeenth century,
engaged in a critical investigation into textual variants. In 1734 Johann
Bengel (Tübingen) issued a critical text, not exactly the *textus receptus*,
and is regarded as important for modern scientific textual criticism because of his principles (e.g., the more difficult reading is preferred) and
theories of manuscript families (groupings of manuscripts). Johann
Wettstein's Greek New Testament (1751-52, Amsterdam) contained
many important (new) variants. Johann Griesbach (text, 1774-75) agreed
with Bengel on the grouping of manuscript families. His theories have
lived on in textual criticism (e.g., a reading must have an ancient witness, the shorter as well as the more difficult is preferred).

And so on went the reception of the *textus receptus* until 1831,
when Karl Lachmann set it aside and published a text based entirely on
ancient manuscripts. (In 1881, Westcott and Hort published *The New
Testament in the Original Greek*, which has become in effect a new *textus
receptus*.)

Textual criticism, with the thousands and thousands of manuscripts
and the tens of thousands of variant readings, was complicated not only
by the discipline itself but also by the tradition (Church) that has received the biblical text. Critical interpretation of the text developed
earlier under the aegis of rationalism. Critical rendering of the text itself was slower to develop not only because Erasmus' text was based on

THE HISTORY OF SCRIPTURE IN THE CHURCH

late evidence but also because it has seldom been regarded as purely a scientific task.

4. Historical consciousness. What developed in Humanism, a sense of historical distance from the past, including Scripture, continued to develop in the early modern period with all the critical methodologies.

Historical consciousness, or the dawning thereof, is part and parcel of what we have been discussing. The problem of hermeneutics as the problem of understanding and language is brought into the nineteenth century by Friedrich Schleiermacher and beyond our scope. Hermeneutics as the problem of expression, interpretation, and translation is brought into focus in the early modern period with the rise of the historical-critical method. Key in this development is the separation between text and reader, namely the consciousness of the separation.

One way of describing this development is to use the distinction between internalization and externalization used in the sociology of knowledge. In the medieval-early Reformation period, as our argument has gone, the reader internalized Scripture, morning, noon, and night. With Humanism—printing, editing, translating, introducing—developed the externalization of the Bible as an ancient text. The concern of methodology is to find the way(s) of bridging the gap between text and interpreter. Once interpretation (with historical consciousness) becomes the focus of biblical study, then the Orthodox needed to set up a system, with logical coherence, to make the Lutheran interpretation correct one vis-à-vis the Roman and the Reformed traditions. The emancipator from Orthodox dogmatism is always described as reason (and on to rationalism). But Orthodoxy used philosophy, and Pietism contributed another crucial element in the emancipation—the subjective experience of the individual. So this perspective suggests that orthodox philosophy plus pietist individualism helped create the atmosphere for rationalism, where the externalization process is advanced. The Bible is to be treated as any other ancient document, in need of historical introduction and linguistic-literary analysis. The distance and task is enormous.

Biblical theology belongs to the ancient world. Dogmatic theology, conscious of its methodology and distance from Scripture, is part of the Church's tradition, also past. If there is to be a bridge between biblical theology and contemporary thinking, it is the task of hermeneutics (translation, interpretation, understanding) to bridge the gulf—and on to the problems of the nineteenth century.

It is with historical consciousness that problems are perceived that were not before—method, exegesis, critical text, interpretation, and hermeneutics—all with the positive use of reason. The rise of the historical-critical method itself is a historical phenomenon. Its posture today is that it is purely objective and scientific. It did not begin that way nor develop untouched by human historical elements. Practitioners of the historical-critical method may want to use the method on itself and see it in its historical setting, which this essay has tried to set out with pure objectivity. The usual survey of the historical-critical method is described with "advance" language, not totally absent from the foregoing. As one author put it, going through the centuries, "It finally won out!" What did it win, outside of control of academic biblical studies? Did it win any new or better or clearer understanding of the text that was unavailable to St. Augustine, Thomas, Luther, or Calvin?

RECOMMENDED READINGS

Aldridge, John W. *The Hermeneutic of Erasmus*. Richmond: John Knox, 1966. Basic level; concentrates on the philosophy of Christ, erudition, and philology.

Cambridge History of the Bible, 3 volumes. Cambridge: University Press, 1963-70. Reference volumes by specialists that cover the early period (I), medieval (II), and modern (III).

Grant, Robert. *A Short History of the Interpretation of the Bible*. New York: Macmillan, 1963; 2nd edition with David Tracy, Philadelphia: Fortress, 1984. Basic introduction that starts with the Bible itself.

Hagen, Kenneth. *Luther's Approach to Scripture as seen in his "Commentaries" on Galatians*. Tübingen: J. C. B. Mohn [Paul Siebeck], 1993. Places Luther in the context of the whole history of biblical interpretation.

Hahn, Herbert F. *The Old Testament in Modern Research*. Philadelphia: Fortress Press, 1954/66. Extensive survey of Old Testament criticism; strong on the moderns.

Kooiman, Willen J. *Luther and the Bible*. Translated by John Schmidt. Philadelphia: Muhlenberg, 1961. Introductory level aimed at a broad coverage of many facets.

Kümmel, Werner G. *The New Testament: The History of the Investigation of its Problems*. Translated by S. M. Gilmour and H. C. Kee. Nashville: Abingdon, 1972. Extensive survey of New Testament criticism; several primary sources. Emphasis on the moderns.

de Lubac, Henri. *The Sources of Revelation*. Translated by L. O'Neill. New York: Herder and Herder, 1968. An abridgment of his monumental work in French on patristic and medieval exegesis; emphasis on the spiritual understanding of Scripture.

Smalley, Beryl. *The Study of the Bible in the Middle Ages*. Oxford: Blackwell, 1952. Scholarly and readable history from the Fathers of the Church to the friars of the thirteenth century.

Stuhlmacher, Peter. *Historical Criticism and Theological Interpretation of Scripture*. Translated by R. Harrisville. Philadelphia: Fortress, 1977. Short overview from the ancients to the twentieth century; reconstruction of the current dilemma.

CATHOLIC INTERPRETATION OF SCRIPTURE
by
Daniel J. Harrington, S.J.

I. The Bible in Catholic Life Today

A friend who by upbringing and conviction is an evangelical Christian made a comment some time ago that startled me. He said that whenever he has had occasion to attend Roman Catholic liturgies recently, he has been struck by how "Protestant" they sounded. He meant that as a compliment, and he went on to explain that what makes him feel at home in Catholic worship today is the massive dose of biblical language—not only in the readings taken directly from the Scriptures but also in the songs and the prayers. His comment led me, as a professional biblical scholar who also preaches and presides regularly at worship services in the Catholic church, to reflect on a dramatic development in my own church.

The foundations for this development were already laid in the 1940s and 1950s by Pope Pius XII's encyclical on biblical studies (*Divino Afflante Spiritu*) and his revision of the liturgical services for Holy Week. But the decisive turning point was the Second Vatican Council. Building upon the directives approved by Pope Pius XII and worked out in more detail by biblical scholars and theologians, the Council Fathers affirmed in a powerful way the importance of the Bible in the life of the Catholic church.

Before we look at the key document relating to the Bible from Vatican II, it may be useful to contrast the place of the Bible in the Catholic church before the Council and its place today. The three areas for contrast are liturgy, theological education, and ecumenism.

Prior to Vatican II, Scripture was certainly an integral part of the Mass. A selection from a New Testament epistle or the Old Testament, as well as a passage from one of the Gospels, was read at every eucharistic service. The priest read these biblical selections in Latin, while some of the laity followed along with the help of an English translation. On Sundays, the passages were also read aloud in English, either as an accompaniment to the Latin or after it. The range of Scripture readings was narrow and repetitive. Matthew's Gospel with its emphases on church order and Petrine authority was especially prominent.

Vatican II removed the language barrier by decreeing that the sacred liturgy could now be celebrated in modern languages as well as Latin. The Bible is now read in English (or whatever language is most appropriate), and the readings have a very prominent place. Shortly after the council, the liturgists worked out a new and more comprehensive cycle of Scripture readings. For Sundays there is a three-year cycle, each Sunday having passages from the Old Testament, the book of Psalms, the New Testament Epistles, and the Gospels. For weekdays there is a two-year cycle consisting of a passage from the Old Testament or the New Testament Epistles, a psalm, and the Gospels. This development means that in their worship services, Catholics today are exposed to large amounts of Scripture in the language that they most readily understand.

Prior to Vatican II, the Bible was not ordinarily read directly as part of the primary- or secondary-school program in religious education. In Catholic colleges, the study of the Bible was supplemented by conservative textbooks that guided students along approved paths. In the training of Catholic priests, biblical courses were usually placed at the end of the program, after the proper dogmatic theological foundations were already in place. Professors of Scripture in pre-Vatican II seminaries were generally very cautious not to stray into the realms of dogmatic theology or moral theology. They focused on philological and historical matters. What they taught were officially classified as "minor courses."

Vatican II made clear that biblical studies are central in Catholic theology. In the many years that I have taught in Catholic seminaries since 1971, I have never heard a student question or complain about the need for Scripture courses. These courses are taken at the beginning, middle, and end of seminary programs. The students work hard at these courses and enjoy them. The professors dialogue with and even teach courses with their colleagues in systematic and moral theology. At every level in the Catholic educational system—colleges, high schools, grammar schools, religious education classes—the Bible is read and discussed. Catholics are becoming increasingly familiar with the language and themes of Scripture and thus better able to appreciate their language of worship.

My Protestant friend's comment about the more "biblical" character of Catholic life raises the issue about the ecumenical significance of the Bible for Catholics. Prior to Vatican II, many Catholics looked upon the Bible as a "Protestant" book. Those Catholics who read it were careful to follow officially approved handbooks and commentaries and loyally defended the need for such authoritative guidance from the teaching offices of the church. Those who quoted the Bible except to affirm traditional theological positions were considered peculiar or even dangerous.

Vatican II has encouraged Catholics to claim the Bible as their own book. On local, national, and international levels, the Bible has emerged as the common ground for Catholics and Protestants. Both groups have become sensitive to their shared heritage in Scripture and have recognized that many of their sharpest differences come from postbiblical developments. These differences are real and touch on genuine issues but must not obscure what Catholics and Protestants hold in common.

Within Catholic circles there is great enthusiasm for courses and lectures on the Bible. Books about the Bible and translations of the Bible are big sellers. A whole industry of lectures on the Bible that are available in the form of cassettes has sprung up. All these developments show that Catholics now look upon the Bible as "their" book too, see it as a means toward Christian unity, and want to know as much about it as they can.

A very concrete instance of the ecumenical possibility and power of the Bible is the fact that when the new Catholic lectionary was prepared in response to Vatican II, it was adopted (with minor modifications) by several mainline Protestant churches—Lutheran, Episcopal, Methodist, and Presbyterian. This means that on almost every Sunday the same set of Scripture readings is read and preached upon in all these Christian communities. The historical and theological differences between these groups remain, but at least they are dealing with the same basic texts of the Bible.

II. VATICAN II'S CONSTITUTION ON DIVINE REVELATION

The most compact and authoritative statement on the theory and theology of the Bible's place in the Catholic church is Vatican II's Constitution on Divine Revelation (known also by its Latin title *Dei Verbum*. All quotations are from A. Flannery, ed., *Vatican Council II: The Conciliar and Post Conciliar Documents*, 750-65.) That document was issued in November 1965, but the way had been prepared for it by Pope Pius XII's 1943 encyclical *Divino Afflante Spiritu* and by several other official statements through the years. The conciliar document summarized the important points in those earlier statements and pushed Catholic biblical study out of some old ruts and onto better paths.

The first chapter of the six chapters in the Constitution deals with "divine revelation itself." Before the Council and even in the early stages of the drafting of the document, there had been a lively debate about the nature of divine revelation, with many theologians (in the wake of Vatican I's insistence on the content of faith) stressing the primacy of the theological propositions revealed in the Bible. Without denying the content of revelation and its propositional dimension, the final draft of the Council's Constitution stresses the primacy of God's revelation of himself as a person in relationship to his people. The personal dimension of revelation makes possible the propositional dimension: "By divine revelation God wished to manifest and communicate both himself and the eternal decrees of his will concerning the salvation of mankind" (§6). Both dimensions are clearly affirmed, but the personal aspect of revelation is given first place.

The second chapter, which concerns the transmission of divine revelation, takes up the problem of the relation between Scripture and tradition. Rejecting the idea that Scripture and tradition constitute two distinct sources of revelation, the Constitution insisted that they flow from "the same divine well-spring" (§9). It went on to state that "sacred tradition and sacred Scripture make up a single sacred deposit of the Word of God, which is entrusted to the church" (§10). This emphasis on the unity of Scripture and tradition does not simply absorb the latter into the former: "The church does not draw her certainty about all revealed truths from the holy Scriptures alone" (§9). And the task of "giving an authentic interpretation" of both Scripture and tradition is entrusted to "the living teaching office of the church alone" (§10), though it is clearly stated that the ecclesiastical magisterium is "not superior to the Word of God, but is its servant" (§10). Thus the Constitution presents Scripture and tradition as one source of divine revelation while affirming the existence of tradition and making the ecclesiastical magisterium (the Pope and the bishops) the ultimate arbiter.

The third chapter is devoted to divine inspiration and its interpretation. The fact of inspiration is stated at the outset: "The divinely revealed realities, which are contained and presented in the text of sacred Scripture, have been written down under the inspiration of the Holy Spirit" (§11). The same section presents a doctrine of the inerrancy of Scripture: "The books of Scripture, firmly, faithfully, and without error, teach that truth which God, for the sake of our salvation, wished to see confided to the sacred Scriptures." This may sound like a statement of limited inerrancy; that is, only what pertains to our salvation, and not historical or scientific matters, in the Bible is free from error. But, in fact, the theologians who wrote this document and the Council Fathers who voted their approval deliberately sought to avoid approving either complete inerrancy or limited inerrancy as the church's teaching. Since the Constitution was not a theological treatise and since the Council Fathers did not want to absolutize or give official sanction to one theologian or one school, there is no attempt to explain in detail *how* inspiration and inerrancy function or what scope these terms might have. It was more a matter of reaffirming venerable theological teachings without specifying which interpretation of them is best.

The section on the interpretation of Scripture (§12) is the most important part for biblical scholars. Taking its cue from *Divino Afflante Spiritu*, the Constitution urged biblical scholars and indeed all Catholics (1) to pay attention to the literary forms in which divine revelation is expressed, (2) to look to the meaning that the biblical author intended in his own historical situation and culture, and (3) to consider the customary and characteristic patterns of perception, speech, and narrative prevailing at that time. Since this part of the document summarizes so well the tasks undertaken by Catholic biblical scholars, it deserves to be quoted in full:

> In determining the intention of the sacred writers, attention must be paid, *inter alia*, to "literary forms, for the fact is that truth is differently presented and expressed in the various types of historical writing, in prophetical and poetical texts," and in other forms of literary expression. Hence the exegete must look for that meaning which the sacred writer, in a determined situation and given the circumstances of his time and culture, intended to express and did in fact express, through the medium of a contemporary literary form. Rightly to understand what the sacred author wanted to affirm in his work, due attention must be paid both to the customary and characteristic patterns of perception, speech and narrative which prevailed at the age of the sacred writer, and to the conventions which the people of his time followed in their dealings with one another.

The freedom of research expressed in this paragraph is somewhat tempered by a reminder that biblical interpretation is "ultimately subject

to the judgment of the church which exercises the divinely conferred
commission and ministry of watching over and interpreting the word
of God" (§12). The connection between the doctrine of the divine inspiration of Scripture and the task of interpreting Scripture in its
historical context is drawn by using the formula "the words of God,
expressed in the words of men" (§13).

In the fourth chapter, the Constitution defends the divinely inspired character and lasting value of the Old Testament (§14). It does so
by alluding to some of the ways in which the Old Testament has been
viewed in Christian theology: preparation for and prophecy of the coming of Christ, a source for understanding God and his dealings with his
people, and a storehouse of sublime teaching on God and of sound
wisdom on human life (§15). It also mentions that the books of the Old
Testament contain "matters imperfect and provisional," without specifying what these are (cultic rules, calls for vengeance, ethically
questionable actions?) and what Catholics are to do with them. Again
it is important to remember that the Constitution is not a theology
textbook but rather a statement of directions agreed upon and approved
by the Catholic bishops of the world.

The chapter on the New Testament strikes a cautious balance between recognition of the complex process by which the four Gospels
came into being and affirmation of the basic truth of their portraits of
Jesus:

> Holy Mother Church has firmly and with absolute constancy main-
> tained and continues to maintain, that the four Gospels just named,
> whose historicity she unhesitatingly affirms, faithfully hand on what
> Jesus, the Son of God, while he lived among men, really did and taught
> for their eternal salvation, until the day when he was taken up (see
> Acts 1:1-2). For, after the ascension of the Lord, the apostles handed
> on to their hearers what he had said and done, but with that fuller
> understanding which they, instructed by the glorious events of Christ
> and enlightened by the Spirit of truth, now enjoyed. The sacred au-
> thors, in writing the four Gospels, selected certain of the many
> elements which had been handed on, either orally or already in writ-
> ten form, others they synthesized or explained with an eye to the
> situation of the churches, the while sustaining the form of preaching,
> but always in such a fashion that they have told us the honest truth
> about Jesus. Whether they relied on their own memory and recollec-
> tions or on the testimony of those who "from the beginning were
> eyewitnesses and ministers of the Word," their purpose in writing

was that we might know the "truth" concerning the things of which we have been informed (see Luke 1:2-4).

This statement in section 19 leaves room and indeed encourages biblical scholars to do research on the literary forms, sources, and final editing of the Gospels. But it demands that they not lose sight of the historical person of Jesus of Nazareth—the one to whom the Gospels bear witness. The Pauline epistles and the New Testament writings are said to formulate more precisely the authentic teaching of Christ, preach the saving power of his divine work, and foretell its glorious consummation (§20).

The sixth chapter, which deals with sacred Scripture in the life of the Church, provides the directions that have brought about the biblical renewal of recent years. The opening statement in section 21 stresses the link between the Scriptures and the eucharistic body of Christ. Far from separating the two, the Constitution speaks of "the one table of the word of God and the body of Christ." It insists that "all the preaching of the church . . . should be nourished and ruled by sacred Scripture" (§21), that access to Scripture "ought to be wide open to the Christian faithful" (§22), and that study of the "sacred page should be the very soul of sacred theology" (§24). Thus the post-Vatican II developments with respect to the Bible's place in the life of the Church are best seen as faithful responses to the spirit of the Council, not as deviations from it or as a new movement apart from it. If any doubt remained about the central role of biblical studies in the seminary curriculum and the piety of the Church's ministers, the next-to-last section of the Constitution speaks very clearly: "All clerics, particularly priests of Christ and others who, as deacons or catechists, are officially engaged in the ministry of the word, should immerse themselves in the Scriptures by constant sacred reading and diligent study" (§25).

Vatican II's Constitution on Divine Revelation has given important and fruitful directions to the biblical movement in the Catholic church. The most significant directions are summarized by the following list: the emphasis on God's personal revelation as the basis for whatever propositional revelation may be contained in Scripture, the insistence that Scripture and tradition flow from "the same divine wellspring," the forthright acceptance of the historical and literary study of the Scriptures, the respect for the Old Testament, the cautious balance between the complexity of our Gospels and their essential truth about

Jesus, and the encouragement for Bible reading and study in every phase of the Church's life.

There is much on this list with which evangelical and Lutheran Christians can agree, though their emphases may be slightly different. But some evangelicals might take exception to what might appear to be a doctrine of limited inerrancy expressed in the Constitution: "that truth which God, for the sake of our salvation, wished to see confided to the sacred Scriptures" (§11). Both evangelicals and Lutherans will no doubt take strong exception to the idea of the ecclesiastical magisterium as the final arbiter of biblical interpretation (§§10, 12). They may also be skeptical about how well Catholics can manage to keep together Scripture and tradition on the one hand, and word and sacrament on the other hand. But however valid their objections may be, Protestants who take the trouble to read Vatican II's Constitution on Divine Revelation cannot fail to recognize the "biblical" character of much of the language used in the document and the many direct references to Scripture throughout it. The Council Fathers opted for the language of the Bible rather than for the language of scholastic theology.

III. THE WAYS OF CURRENT BIBLICAL SCHOLARSHIP

Up to this point we have considered the practical impact of biblical study on Church life and an official statement about the place of the Bible in the Church. Now is the time to focus on the methods used by Catholic biblical scholars; that is, what those men and women who devote themselves to research on the Scriptures do when they confront the biblical texts.

"Catholic biblical research" is obviously research done by Catholic scholars. Until recently, most biblical professionals were also ordained priests who taught in seminaries or on one of the international biblical faculties in Rome (Pontifical Biblical Institute) or Jerusalem (École Biblique, Studium Biblicum Franciscanum). Since Vatican II, an increasing number of Catholic laymen and laywomen (as well as women religious) have obtained doctoral degrees in biblical studies and are now teaching at Catholic (and other) universities and publishing books and articles. These lay professors are not as immediately under ecclesiastical authority as priests are, but up to this point no great conflict has arisen regarding this matter.

Catholic biblical scholars bring to the text of Scripture the set of concerns and procedures that has been developed over the centuries among serious students of the Bible. In modern times this set of concerns is often called the historical-critical method. This approach takes as its primary task the understanding of the biblical text in its own time and on its own terms. It applies the powers of the mind to the text in order to understand it better and to appreciate it for itself. The major concerns of Catholic biblical scholarship can be presented under ten headings.

1. Literary Criticism.

The Bible is basically an anthology of writings that bear witness to God's dealings with his people. In the Old Testament there are narratives, law codes, prophetic oracles, psalms, and wisdom books. In the New Testament there are stories of Jesus (the four Gospels) and the early church (Acts) as well as epistles by Paul and other figures and an apocalypse (Revelation). Within these large literary types, there are also smaller forms such as sayings, parables, and exhortations. The Bible is most obviously a collection of pieces of literature, and so the obvious starting point for any biblical scholar is literary criticism.

Literary criticism means applying to Scripture the questions and concerns used in the study of any literature. The aim behind the literary-critical approach to the Bible is not to reduce it to the level of other books, but rather to help us appreciate the ways in which the biblical writers communicated to their original audiences and still communicate to us today.

The first concern of literary criticism is the words and images of the texts—the raw materials out of which any written communication is constructed. What does this or that word mean? Is the word being used literally or metaphorically? What symbolism is present in the passage? Then in a narrative text we want to know how the words are put together to form a story and how the characters in the story are related to one another. In a discourse or an epistle the literary critic focuses on the progress of thought—how the words and images are put together to form an argument or move people to good action. Obviously the literary critic proceeds from individual words and images to the coherence of the whole passage and then back to the words and images in light of the whole. The circularity inherent in the study of literature suggests that a text is always capable of receiving better and more adequate readings at various levels of understanding.

Literary critics are also concerned with the literary form of a text. The larger forms, or genres, in the New Testament are familiar: Gospels, Acts, Epistles, and Apocalypse. But within these larger forms the individual parts use vehicles like parables or proverbs or blessings and curses. The now familiar saying that "the medium is the message" makes the point that the choice of a specific literary mode of communication already begins the process of communication. The choice of the literary form of the personal résumé in the United States today communicates that the person is seeking a job. If the job applicant were to present the personnel manager with a poem or a video, the only hope for getting the job would be the display of ingenuity. Therefore, those who study Scripture from the perspective of literary criticism must attend to the literary forms used in the text and how the literary forms contribute to the expression of the message or content.

In one sense, literary criticism is the most basic approach to the biblical text and all the other methods are really specialized operations within this general method. But literary criticism in the narrow sense concentrates on the aesthetic appreciation of the biblical text as literature. Catholic biblical scholars generally have good literary educations and are naturally attracted to relating developments in literary criticism and literary theory to Scripture. The topic of many recent doctoral dissertations and journal articles by Catholics has been the literary outline or structure of a particular passage or biblical book. The dynamics and rhetorical techniques of narratives and the argument structure of the epistles have also been investigated by Catholic (and other) scholars. In parts of Europe and to some extent in the United States, Catholic scholars have tried to use structuralist analysis to understand biblical texts—that is, to go beneath the surface structures of the text and arrive at the deep structures of mind and reality. Others use the approach of deconstruction, which looks on the text as mainly an occasion for creative interpretation.

The literary-critical work of Catholic biblical scholars is part of a larger movement in biblical scholarship that seeks a better appreciation of the Bible as story. This movement has also generated a broader theological approach—the so-called narrative theology or theology of story.

The chief problem connected with the literary approach is its tendency to reduce everything to textual aesthetics. Since the methods for interpreting fiction or poetry work well on various sections of Scripture, some conclude that everything in Scripture is fiction or poetry and thus without historical significance. Such a conclusion clearly goes beyond the boundaries of the Constitution on Divine Revelation and of Catholic theology in general. But it also raises an interesting question: If one admits the Old Testament books of Jonah, Tobit, Esther, and Judith are literary fictions (and most Catholic biblical scholars take this approach—a correct approach, in my opinion), where does one draw the line between literary fiction and biblical history? This is a serious problem, but it should not obscure or detract from the very positive results that emerge from bringing to the text of Scripture the concerns and methods of literary criticism and appreciating the Bible as literature.

2. **Textual Criticism.**
    Since words are the materials out of which literary texts are constructed, it is essential to be as sure as possible about the accuracy of the words in the texts. The biblical texts have been handed on through the centuries and thus have been subject to distortion and human error. The goal of textual criticism is to get back as close as possible to what the biblical writers set down in their original manuscripts.
    Reaching that goal is not easy. Textual critics must work with the Hebrew, Aramaic, and Greek manuscripts of the Bible. They must also make use of the earliest translations into Aramaic, Greek, Latin, Syriac, Ethiopic, Armenian, etc. Prior to the discovery of biblical manuscripts among the Dead Sea Scrolls at Qumran, the earliest available Hebrew manuscripts of the Old Testament were from the tenth and eleventh centuries A.D. The most important manuscripts of the New Testament came from the fourth and fifth centuries A.D., though there are some fragmentary manuscripts (the so-called papyri) from the second and third centuries. So textual critics must learn many ancient languages and prepare themselves to work with manuscripts far removed in time from the originals.
    Having assembled the manuscript evidence, textual critics compare the texts to uncover textual variants. These variants are then weighed in order to determine on rational grounds what was the reading of the original text and what crept into the tradition as the result of conscious or unconscious alteration. In making such decisions, textual critics must take into account the quantity and quality of the manuscript evidence (external evidence) as well as the context, language, and style of the document (internal evidence). The task of the textual critic

of the Bible is lightened somewhat by the general reliability of the process of transmission and the abundance of manuscript evidence.

A large amount of that manuscript evidence is preserved at the Vatican Library in Rome and in other libraries and monasteries of the Catholic church. These manuscripts are accessible to all scholars either for direct inspection or by photographic reproductions. Indeed the institutional structures of the Catholic church throughout the ages have made possible the transmission of the New Testament text from generation to generation, and our knowledge of the Old Testament tradition would be far poorer without these institutions.

Modern Catholic biblical scholars are well prepared for textual criticism through a good grounding in ancient languages. Nevertheless, few are prominent in this discipline. An important exception was Carlo M. Martini, an Italian Jesuit who was a member of an international and interconfessional panel charged with preparing a new standard edition of the Greek New Testament. But he is now the Cardinal Archbishop of Milan, and his pastoral duties leave him no time for textual criticism. In a similar project for preparing a new edition of the Hebrew Old Testament, the Dominican scholar Dominique Barthélemy is a major figure. Several American Jesuits have worked with Frank M. Cross of Harvard in his reevaluation of Old Testament textual criticism in light of the Qumran discoveries.

The question remains: Why are so few Catholic scholars prominent in this discipline? The reason is clearly not lack of education, especially in the languages. One can only speculate on this matter, but perhaps one factor is a lack of the Protestant passion for discovering the exact wording of the original manuscript as it came from the hand of the biblical writer. Many evangelicals limit biblical inspiration to the so-called autographs (the manuscripts written by the biblical writer), and so there is a powerful religious motive to get back to the original texts. The Catholic doctrine of inspiration is not so narrow and places more trust in the process of transmission. Thus the divergent understandings of biblical inspiration may well be a factor, here, though there are surely other factors: the pastoral demands made on Catholic clerics, the so-called "twentieth-century interlude" in New Testament textual criticism, and the intrinsically difficult and often tedious nature of the research.

3. **The World of the Bible.**
The heavy emphasis on biblical languages in the training of Catholic scholars finds expression most dramatically in research on the world of the Bible, especially on the texts discovered in the Middle East during the past two hundred years. These texts have allowed us to leap back over the centuries and to see what terms, ideas, and customs were in the background of the biblical writings.

For the Old Testament, the most important extrabiblical texts are in Semitic languages such as Akkadian, Aramaic, and Ugaritic, as well as Sumerian and Egyptian. These texts have illumined our understanding of the creation stories in Genesis, the historical setting of the biblical narratives from earliest times to the postexilic period, and the language and literary form of the Psalms. For the New Testament, the most significant ancient texts are in Hebrew, Aramaic, Greek, Latin, and Coptic (Nag Hammadi documents). These texts have shed light on the eschatological consciousness of the early Christians and the emergence of the early church, the cultural milieu(s) in which Christianity developed, and some of the problems and threats that it faced.

Many of these discoveries are so recent that they have still not been assimilated into biblical commentaries. When they are, it is crucial for the exegete to make clear what elements the biblical and extrabiblical texts share and where they differ. It is also important to specify the historical relationships between the two texts. Obviously the best parallels are those between texts from roughly the same time and place, for then we have a better chance of knowing what was "in the air."

The Biblical Institute Press of the Pontifical Biblical Institute in Rome has played a leading role in the editing and publishing of textual material from the ancient Near East. Many dissertations by Catholic scholars in Rome and elsewhere have been explorations of biblical texts in light of extrabiblical material. The professors at the Dominican École Biblique in Jerusalem have been active participants in publishing the Qumran scrolls and in the archaeological excavations at Qumran and elsewhere. The faculty and students of the Studium Biblicum Franciscanum have made many contributions in the archaeology of early Christianity and in exploring the phenomenon of Jewish Christianity. Catholic scholars have been prominent in editing the texts from Ugarit, Qumran, and Nag Hammadi. The fact that many older Catholic scholars were well versed in the Greek and Latin classics has meant that the Greco-Roman setting of early Christianity has remained a lively field of research.

The great interest of Catholic scholars in the world of the Bible and in texts from antiquity in particular may stem in part from the perennial Catholic fascination with the relation between religion and culture. Catholic theology emphasizes the idea that God expresses himself in the midst of created realities and human culture. If this is so in the present, it must also have been so in antiquity when the books of the Bible were being composed. Therefore, the more that scholarship can reveal about the realities and culture of the biblical world, the richer and deeper will our understanding of the Bible be. My hunch is that this theological emphasis underlies much of the scientific research done by Catholic scholars on the world of the Bible.

4. Word Study.

The serious training in biblical languages that is demanded of Catholic scholars also shows itself in their research on the words and ideas in Scripture. The archaeological discoveries of recent years have brought forth many ancient texts, and those texts have greatly illumined our understanding of the languages of the Bible (Hebrew, Aramaic, and Greek). In Old Testament research, the Ugaritic texts from Ras-Shamra have revolutionized the study of Hebrew poetry, and the legal and mythic texts in Akkadian have made more intelligible various customs and terms in the Pentateuch. New Testament scholars have learned much about the kind of Greek used in Jesus' time from the Egyptian papyri and about the terminology and thought of Jewish apocalypticism from the Dead Sea Scrolls.

The most common kind of word study in the biblical field usually begins with a particularly important or problematic passage. In order to get a better understanding of a difficult word or idea in the target passage, the scholar makes a survey of the instances of the term in other documents. If a New Testament word is under consideration, then one looks at the Greek writings of the classical authors, the Greek translation of the Old Testament (Septuagint), and the Jewish authors Philo and Josephus. Naturally one also searches out the Hebrew Old Testament, the Dead Sea scrolls, and other relevant documents. In each occurrence of the word, the focus of research is what it means in its context in the hope of understanding better the target passage.

In addition to the extrabiblical evidence, word study must also take into account parallels within the Bible itself. In this step an important change has taken place in Catholic biblical scholarship in recent years. In the past there was a tendency to join together all the biblical instances of a term or idea as if the Bible were made out of whole cloth. The theological assumption was that the Bible is a unity and that its language is a special type of Hebrew or Greek ("Holy Ghost Greek"). Now the major concern among Catholic scholars is to let the distinct accents within the Bible be heard. Their emphasis is on plurality of views within Scripture and on the particular contributions of the individual writers.

The phrase "biblical theology" is popular in Catholic circles, and a very common way of doing biblical theology is to trace the history of a word or idea from earliest Old Testament times, through intertestamental Jewish writings and classic works, to the New Testament. The aim is to see both continuity and decisive shifts in meaning; the conclusion to such studies usually involves a synthesis and an assessment of challenges for the Church today. This kind of study places detailed philological research on individual biblical and extrabiblical texts in the broader framework of the history of biblical ideas.

Part of the popularity of this approach to biblical theology among Catholic scholars is due to the Catholic concern and fondness for tradition. This approach is really a charting out of the tradition of a biblical word or idea. For a church that is immersing itself more and more in language and ideas of Scripture, and that is so eager to hand on the tradition of faith, the concentration on key concepts and their development in biblical times and against the background of the biblical world is a sound approach and is sure to pay rich rewards.

5. Source Criticism.

The task of detecting where a source was used in a biblical book is called "source criticism." Sometimes we are told explicitly by the biblical author that he was using a source, and so the procedure is quite simple. The more difficult instances are those in which the use of a source is suspected but needs to be proved by rational analysis. The internal criteria for determining the presence of a source in the Bible (or in any other text) include the following: vocabulary in a passage different from everything else in the book, a shift in tone or literary style, an unexpected interruption in the context and an awkward resumption of it later, the presence of the same story twice in slightly different forms, and theological or ideological contradictions within the same book.

The most important areas of source criticism in biblical research concern the Pentateuch and the synoptic Gospels. The classic four-document hypothesis used in explaining the origin of the first five books of the Old Testament claims that Pentateuch is the fusion of four sources: Yahwist (J), Elohist (E), Priestly (P), and Deuteronomist (D). The time span from the earliest document (J) to the latest (P) is about four hundred years (950 B.C. to 550 B.C.). The classic two-source hypothesis of the synoptic Gospels maintains that Mark was the earliest Gospel (ca. A.D. 70) and that Matthew and Luke (ca. A.D. 80-90) used both Mark and a collection of Jesus' sayings known among modern scholars as Q (ca. A.D. 50).

These hypotheses were popularized in liberal Protestant circles in nineteenth-century Germany. The initial Catholic responses were generally suspicious and negative. But as the arguments and their proponents were gradually separated, there was increasing acceptance—to the point that both of these hypotheses are now part of "scholarly orthodoxy" among Catholic biblical scholars. In the broader context of biblical scholarship, both source-hypotheses are under attack, and Catholics can be found on the various sides of the debate. But there is some irony in the fact that the modern stronghold of the classic two-source hypothesis of the synoptic Gospels is the Catholic University of Louvain in Belgium.

6. **Redaction Criticism.**

Where it has been possible to isolate sources on external or internal grounds, the way is cleared for redaction criticism—the exegetical method that focuses on the particular emphases or views that the biblical writers have imposed on their sources. Besides the literary task of determining the final writer or redactor's distinctive contributions, redaction criticism also involves a historical task since the redactor's emphases and views can shed light on his situation within the early church and on the problems that the redactor and his community were facing.

It is possible to apply the techniques of redaction criticism to any part of Scripture, but the most fertile ground for redaction criticism has been the synoptic Gospels. The pioneers of the redaction-critical approach to Gospel study (Günther Bornkamm, Hans Conzelmann, Willi Marxsen) were German Protestant scholars but their work in the late 1940s and 1950s was taken up with great enthusiasm by Catholic scholars in the 1960s and 1970s. In one sense, the approach has been "played out," since practically every Gospel text has been the object of close redaction-critical analysis. On the other hand, the concern with the final redaction of biblical books has become so integral a part of the exegetical task that no commentator can disregard it.

As I have already observed, redaction criticism is popular among Catholic biblical scholars. This is so in part because Catholic scholars are part of the international and interconfessional dialogue of biblical research today. But redaction criticism also has had a special attractiveness for Catholics. The approach's understanding of the biblical writers as transmitters and interpreters of tradition strikes a responsive chord among tradition-conscious Catholics. Its interest in early church life and its view of the biblical authors as writing in and for particular communities of faith parallel the perennial Catholic concerns with the Church.

7. Form Criticism.

Under the heading of literary criticism, there was some discussion about the literary forms in which the biblical writers expressed themselves and the extent to which the choice of a particular literary form already communicates some of the writer's message. Thus form criticism is really an aspect of the general literary-critical task, and the first concern of the form critic is to determine the literary form of the book (narrative, letter, etc.) or of the passages within a book (proverb, parable, thanksgiving, etc.). But there is also a historical task in form criticism just as there is in redaction criticism. The assumption is that the particular literary form can tell us something about the community in which the tradition was used and about the problems that the community faced.

Catholic reactions to form criticism have been ambivalent. No one quarrels about the attention paid to literary forms. Indeed the determination of the literary forms has been strongly encouraged since *Divino Afflante Spiritu* (1943) and endorsed enthusiastically in Vatican II's Constitution on Divine Revelation (1965). The ambivalence involves the historical dimension. Catholics are generally positive toward the effort to get behind the texts into the life of the community. In fact, the historical program of form criticism has sometimes even been used apologetically to confirm the Catholic approach to the Bible as the Church's book.

The Catholic problem with form criticism arises from the feeling that it is a poor historical tool. The attempt to construct the history of the early church on form-critical grounds has never been very successful. Where it has been tried, there has usually been a rather undisciplined mixing of form and content to arrive at tendentious (Martin Dibelius's phrase "in the beginning was the sermon") or skeptical conclusions about the relation of the tradition to Jesus of Nazareth (Rudolf Bultmann's history of the Synoptic tradition). The tendency of the form-critical pioneers to overemphasize the creativity of the community at the expense of historical foundations went beyond the boundaries of Catholic theology and was sharply criticized.

8. **Historical Criticism.**
The task of relating the texts of Scripture and the events behind them is called historical criticism. The term "historical-critical method" is generally taken to refer to the whole project of interpreting the biblical text in its historical setting and on its own terms. But "historical criticism" is also used in a more narrow sense to describe the attempt to determine what really happened, for example, at Israel's escape from Egypt or on Easter Sunday morning. It was the hope of "scientific" historians in the nineteenth century to peel away the encrustations of tradition and arrive at the solid core of genuine history. In liberal Protestant circles in Germany there seems to have been an assumption that the goodness of Jesus had been obscured and distorted by Church tradition (including the church of New Testament times).

In his 1898 essay on historical and dogmatic method in theology, the German Protestant theologian Ernst Troeltsch enunciated the three principles of historical criticism. The first was the principle of *criticism* or *methodological doubt*: History only achieves probability, and the religious tradition must be subjected to historical criticism. This first principle presents few problems for Catholic theologians; but the second principle does. According to the principle of *analogy*, present experiences and occurrences are the criteria of probability in the past. That sounds acceptable until one reflects that since dead people do not rise at present, another explanation than what is in the Gospels must be found for the events after Jesus' death. The principle of *correlation* also causes problems for Catholic theology: All historical phenomena are so interrelated that a change in one phenomenon necessitates a change in the causes leading to it and in the effects it has. Such a view of cause and effect again sounds initially acceptable, but a rigid view of it rules out miracles and salvation history (since theological or transcendental causes are not to be involved in historical criticism).

The problems posed by the principles of analogy and correlation are chiefly philosophical, for they presuppose a very different kind of universe from the one assumed in the Bible and the Christian tradition. This is not to say that the philosophical and theological issues raised by these principles are insignificant or can be waved aside by appeal to Scripture. But it is important to recognize that these principles rest on debatable philosophical presuppositions and then are elevated to the status of criteria for judging what really happened in biblical times. It is important also to recognize that Catholic theologians should have no quarrel with historical criticism provided that it does not involve the narrow understanding assumed in Troeltsch's three principles.

Thus the Catholic problem with historical criticism is twofold: (1) Historical criticism has frequently taken a negative view of tradition and Church; (2) historical criticism has frequently been based on unacceptable philosophical assumptions. These problems, however, do not absolve Catholic exegetes from trying to determine what really happened where this might be possible. The theological aberrations of some historical critics do not destroy the validity of the entire historical-critical enterprise.

9. **Translations.**

One very concrete way in which the exegetical labors of Catholic biblical scholars reach the wider church membership is through translations of the Bible. Since Vatican II, it is assumed that Catholic translations will be based on the original languages (Hebrew, Aramaic, Greek) rather than on the Latin Vulgate. The two major English translations prepared under Catholic auspices are the Jerusalem Bible and the New American Bible. They are widely used in liturgical activity and in private reading by English-speaking Catholics.

The English Jerusalem Bible was first published in 1966. In many respects (especially in the introductions and notes) it is dependent on the French *Bible de Jérusalem* (1956). The British team of translators worked with the original languages but generally followed the French translators when questions about variant readings or interpretation arose. The New American Bible (1970) is basically the work of members of the Catholic Biblical Association of America, though not all the collaborators were Catholics. The fact that these two English translations appeared shortly after Vatican II should not disguise the fact that they were already in preparation for many years and constitute an eloquent witness to Catholic biblical scholarship between *Divino Afflante Spiritu* (1943) and Vatican II. Both versions were thoroughly revised in the 1980s—the entire Jerusalem Bible and the New Testament and Psalms of the New American Bible—to reflect developments in scholarship, changes in the English language (especially gender inclusiveness), and the continuing search for accuracy.

There are two philosophies of translation operative in biblical circles these days. A formal equivalence translation (like the Revised Standard Version) aims to be intelligible to people today while mirroring the vocabulary, imagery, and syntax of the original text. A dynamic equivalence translation (like the Good News Bible) is concerned with the total process of communication and seeks to produce the same effect in people today as the biblical authors did among their contemporaries. Taking these two philosophies as the far ends of a spectrum, we can say that the New American Bible tends toward formal equivalence and the Jerusalem Bible leans toward dynamic equivalence. Neither translation is a "pure" representative of a strict philosophy; both manage to embody a good deal of technical biblical scholarship in a modest fashion.

10. Hermeneutics.

The term "hermeneutics" covers the entire process of biblical interpretation that has been explained so far in this part of the essay. But it is sometimes also reserved for the step that takes place after the exegesis has been done and the student of Scripture tries to articulate what the text means. The product may be a scholarly article, a homily, or a popular lecture. Since no one comes to the hermeneutical task without special interests or intellectual history, at this point I would like to call attention to four general characteristics of Catholic biblical scholarship today: its commitment to ecumenism, its sense of tradition, its relation to the Church, and its international dimension.

Biblical scholarship has brought Catholic scholars into contact with people of other religious commitments. Many American Catholic scholars have been trained in languages, history, archaeology, and exegesis at

Johns Hopkins, Harvard, Yale, Chicago, and other such institutions. Catholic scholars play important administrative and editorial roles in the Society of Biblical Literature in the United States, the Society of New Testament Studies, and the Society of Old Testament Studies. For many years, Catholics have worked together with their colleagues, thus contributing to what has become an international and interconfessional dialogue. On the other hand, Catholics have made available their technical biblical journals (*Catholic Biblical Quarterly, Revue Biblique, Biblische Zeitschrift, Biblica, Estudios Biblicos, Rivista Biblica*) to all competent scholars. For many years also, Protestant scholars have given papers at the meetings of the Catholic Biblical Association. This remarkable level of ecumenical cooperation has been carefully fostered by biblical scholars representing the various confessions precisely because they have seen how fruitful and healthy it can be for the Church at large.

Yet the strong commitment to ecumenism by Catholic biblical scholars does not mean a desire to do away with a sense of Catholic tradition. The Catholic church is very much an institution of traditions, and this feature of Catholicism leaves its mark on Catholic biblical scholarship. This tendency shows itself first in typically Catholic approaches to the relation between the earthly Jesus, the early church, and the New Testament writings. While acknowledging the complexity of the Gospel tradition and even delighting in it, the Catholic approach assumes a continuity and rejects the idea of an unbridgeable gulf. The agent in this continuity is the Church under the guidance of the Holy Spirit. The Catholic concern with tradition also manifests itself in a lively interest in philosophy and general hermeneutical theory. There is a strong awareness of the complexity involved in bringing Scripture to bear on church life today and a consciousness that Scripture has been interpreted in various ways at various points in history.

Thirdly, there is a strong sense of Church in Catholic biblical scholarship. The locus for most Catholic biblical scholarship is the Church rather than the academy. The assumption is that biblical exegesis is more than historical research and ought to contribute positively to the church's life. Many issues studied by Catholics—the New Testament divorce texts, ministry in the early church, the role of women—reflect the agenda of church problems today. This strong identification of biblical scholarship with the Church occasionally leads to situations in which the results of exegesis and current church policy appear to col-

lide. An example is the ordination of women to the ministerial priesthood. The conclusion of a group of biblical scholars that Scripture
presents no obstacle to women's ordination was deemed insufficient to
justify departure from tradition by higher Roman authorities. When
such a collision occurs, "pure" exegesis sometimes loses out and is subordinated to tradition and the judgment of the ecclesiastical magisterium
(the Pope and the bishops).

Finally, the international character of the Catholic church is
hermeneutically significant. The network of communication that exists in the Catholic church will not allow North American or Western
European biblical scholars to avoid for long the challenges posed by
Third World exegetes. Indian Catholic scholars have been exploring
the relation between the historical-critical approach to exegesis and the
traditional Indian methods of interpreting religious texts. Latin American biblical theologians have emphasized the centrality of the theme of
liberation, the importance of being conscious of the life-setting of Bible
study, and the political significance of the biblical message in the past
and today. Africans have discerned an affinity between the biblical world
and their own and reject the idea that they must interpret Scripture
through the medium of Western culture. Feminists in the United States
have questioned the usual reconstruction of early Christian history and
found indications of a significant role for women in early church life.
Their feminist concerns and methods are being taken up in turn by
European and African scholars.

By way of contrast here, the method employed by the Latin American theologians of liberation deserves an explanation, for its principles
differ from and challenge the historical-critical approach outlined in
the preceding pages. The starting point for the liberation theologians is
the analysis of contemporary sociopolitical experience, not the investigation of the ancient historical context. The life-setting for this kind of
biblical interpretation is the so-called base community, which arose as
a popular movement in Catholicism. The biblical interpreters, whether
they are peasants or professors, perceive clear parallels between the
situation of people in Latin America today and that of God's people in
biblical times. This parallelism leads back logically to the biblical texts
as sources of enlightenment and encouragement today.

The liberation theologians also challenge the ideal of the historical
critic as the objective spectator or the uninvolved reporter. About thirty
years ago there was a lively debate among European and North Ameri-

can exegetes and theologians about whether it is possible to have presuppositionless exegesis. The answer, of course, is no. But nevertheless the aim of historical criticism is to put aside one's own presuppositions as much as possible and take the text on its own terms. The liberation theologians argue that this pseudo-objective stance merely masks a whole set of hidden and potentially destructive assumptions about God, humanity, and the world. Therefore they call for the interpreter's forthright admission of a political, sociological, or theological position. They criticize bitterly those learned biblical commentaries that issue from professors' desks, apparently untouched by social experience and devoid of human commitment.

The third challenge to historical criticism raised by the liberation theologians involves what constitutes the adequate interpretation of Scripture. The liberation theologians argue that intellectual appropriation is not enough. Neither is prayer enough. Rather, the biblical texts naturally lead to concrete social actions issuing from intellectual reflection and meditation. For these liberation theologians, biblical interpretation necessarily demands sociopolitical activity. Guided by the sophisticated hermeneutical theories of Paul Ricoeur, these liberation theologians speak of a hermeneutical circle that moves from suspicion about present-day experience ("something is wrong"), through suspicion about the ideologies and theologies (and exegesis) that support the present-day political structures, to the Bible as a source of faith and of inspiration for action, to action in the present time.

Thus the Latin American liberation theologians differ from the historical critics in their insistence on the present-day political situation as the starting point for biblical interpretation, their admission of presuppositions, and their emphasis on action as part of the interpretative process. Their approach is clearly open to abuses. But it does illuminate by contrast some of the major features of the historical-critical method. Also, there is still a place for historical criticism in liberation theology. The liberation theologians simply demand that other aspects of the interpretative process—present-day experience, the interpreter's presuppositions, and political action—be acknowledged and celebrated.

IV. FROM DEATH TO LIFE (EPH 2:1-10)

The epistle to the Ephesians purports to be a letter written by Paul from prison. It is often classed with the epistles to the Philippians, Colossians, and Philemon as one of the Captivity Epistles. But most critical Catholic scholars now agree with their Protestant colleagues that Ephesians is an essay written by an admirer of Paul in the late first century A.D. (ca. A.D. 80-90) in order to emphasize the unity in Christ between Jewish Christians and Gentile Christians. The case against Pauline authorship involves the more Semitic language and style of Ephesians, its different use of certain themes and motifs, and its divergent or more developed theology. The development of church structures assumed in the epistle and the problems facing the community are more easily linked with the late first century than the late 50s or early 60s. The hypothesis of non-Pauline authorship no longer presents a serious problem among Catholic exegetes (though a few still argue that Paul was the author).

Ephesians 2:1-10 deals with the reconciliation of sinful humanity to God. It prepares for the discussion of how non-Jews can become part of the people of God (Eph 2:11-22). The Revised New American Bible translates the passage as follows:

> [1]You were dead in your transgressions and sins [2]in which you once lived following the age of this world, following the ruler of the power of the air, the spirit that is now at work in the disobedient. [3]All of us once lived among them in the desires of our flesh, following the wishes of the flesh and the impulses, and we were by nature children of wrath, like the rest. [4]But God, who is rich in mercy, because of the great love he had for us, [5]even when we were dead in our transgressions, brought us to life with Christ (by grace you have been saved), [6]raised us up with him, and seated us with him in the heavens in Christ Jesus, [7]that in the ages to come he might show the immeasurable riches of his grace in his kindness to us in Christ Jesus. [8]For by grace you have been saved through faith, and this is not from you; it is the gift of God; [9]it is not from works, so no one may boast. [10]For we are his handiwork, created in Christ Jesus for the good works that God has prepared in advance, that we should live in them.

The New Jerusalem Bible renders Ephesians 2:1-10 in this way:

> [1]And you were dead, through the crimes and the sins [2]which used to make up your way of life when you were living by the principles of this world, obeying the ruler who dominates the air, the spirit who is at work in those who rebel. [3]We too were all among them once, living only by our natural inclinations, obeying the demands of human self-indulgence and our own whim; our nature made us no less liable to God's retribution than the rest of the world. [4]But God, being rich in faithful love, through the great love with which he loved us, [5]even when we were dead in our sins, brought us to life with Christ—it is

through grace that you have been saved—⁶and raised us up with him and gave us a place with him in heaven, in Christ Jesus. ⁷This was to show for all ages to come, through his goodness towards us in Christ Jesus, how extraordinarily rich he is in grace. ⁸Because it is by grace that you have been saved, through faith; not by anything of your own, but by a gift from God; ⁹not by anything that you have done, so that nobody can claim the credit. ¹⁰We are God's work of art, created in Christ Jesus for the good works which God has already designated to make up our way of life.

This summary of Paul's Gospel first explains the state of sin and spiritual death in which the Gentile Christians lived before Christ (vv. 1-3). By their immoral actions they showed their allegiance to the powers of evil and thus deserved God's anger. Their lord was the "prince of the air," their way of life was guided by the "flesh," and their activities were sins and offenses.

Having described the negative period of their lives, the author of Ephesians develops the positive side in verses 4-10. Through his most powerful display of mercy, love, and grace (vv. 4-5), God in Christ saved these Gentiles from their spiritual death and allowed them to share in the glory of the risen Lord (v. 6). The present aspect or realized aspect of eschatology is strongly emphasized: "you have been saved...he raised us up with him and seated us with him in the heavens." Nevertheless, the future aspect of eschatology ("in the ages to come") is not ignored (v. 7). There is so much emphasis on God in Christ as the source of salvation and the unmerited character of salvation (vv. 8-9) that one can suspect some controversy about this in the background of the letter. The passage closes in verse 10 with an exhortation to live the life that befits those whom God in Christ has saved. The second half of Ephesians (chs. 4-6) spells out what such a life in conformity with salvation means.

I would like to comment on three matters arising from this extraordinarily rich text: its theology, its relationship to the genuine Pauline writings, and its transfer value.

The passage draws a contrast between what life for the Gentile Christians was before Christ (vv. 1-3) and what it is now (vv. 4-10). The most striking theological feature is the emphasis on salvation as already present (vv. 5-6), though the future dimension of salvation is also mentioned (v. 7). In this respect the language of Ephesians is stronger than that of Paul in Romans and Galatians. Another important feature is the stress on the unmerited nature of salvation (vv. 8-9) and the idea of good deeds flowing from God's gift of salvation (v. 10). Even though some Protestants might think that Catholics seek salvation through works, the position of Catholic theology is perfectly consistent with Ephesians on this matter. These two themes—the present dimension of salvation and God's grace as the source of good deeds—would have great appeal to Catholic readers of the Bible.

How would Catholics assess the relationship of this passage to Paul's genuine letters? How would they evaluate the Ephesian emphasis on the presence of salvation in comparison to Paul's stress on the future dimension? Defenders of Pauline authorship of Ephesians would see it as the mature statement of ideas that were germinating in Galatians and Romans. Proponents of pseudonymous authorship would hold that it is an authentic development of Paul's thought for a new situation and time. The idea of using Galatians and Romans as a canon to criticize and judge other canonical writings would not be the usual approach for Catholics. Instead of seizing upon the contradictions and differences, the first instinct of Catholics would be to focus on continuity and development. The aim behind charting the course of a Pauline theme like eschatology would be to illustrate growth in insight and ability to adapt the Gospel to changed circumstances, not to let the power and majesty of the genuine Paul shine forth.

My final comment involves the hermeneutical transfer value of Ephesians 2:1-10. The text was clearly addressed to non-Jews who had turned from paganism to Christian faith. It deals with the experience of conversion ("once . . . but now"). The kind of conversion described implies that the converts were adults when they turned from paganism to Christianity, and in that turning experienced what is called "salvation." If one were to preach on this text today, the audience to whom it would mean most would be adults who had converted from paganism to Christianity. For Catholics and others baptized at infancy, this kind of conversion language is only partially appropriate. Even Christians baptized as adults but having been raised in Christian families and a Christian atmosphere will have not undergone the kind of experience sketched in Ephesians 2:1-10.

The problem of transfer is posed by the language of conversion leading to baptism found in this and other Pauline texts. Very often this conversion language is taken by committed Christians as something to be experienced anew everyday, as delineating the daily life of every Christian. This hermeneutical move transforms conversion language into maintenance language. I hesitate to use the word "distortion" because it is so strong. But at least Christians who use this text today should be aware of its original conversion setting in Ephesians and the only partly justified maintenance application they make of it.

V. SUMMARY

Since the Second Vatican Council, Catholics have been reading the Bible with enthusiasm and making it their own book. This development is especially dramatic in liturgy, religious education, and ecumenism. Vatican II's Constitution on Divine Revelation provided some helpful directions regarding the personal character of divine revelation, Scripture and tradition, the need for interpreting Scripture in its historical setting, respect for the Old Testament, recognition of the complexity of the Gospels, and the Bible's place in church life.

Catholic biblical scholars bring to the Scriptures the questions and concerns that constitute the historical-critical method. They work in the areas of literary criticism, textual criticism, the world of the Bible, word study, source criticism, redaction criticism, form criticism, historical criticism, and translation. In interpreting the Bible, they are committed to ecumenism, maintain a strong sense of Catholic tradition, do their research in the context of today's Church, and are participants in an international dialogue. A "Catholic" reading of Ephesians 2:1-10 emphasizes the present dimension of salvation and God's grace as the source of good actions, sees the passage as an authentic development of Paul's theology, and recognizes the limitations imposed by its original context as adult conversion leading to baptism.

RECOMMENDED READINGS

Bergant, Diane and Robert J. Karris, eds. *The Collegeville Bible Commentary.* Collegeville, MN: Liturgical Press, 1989. This one-volume commentary on both Testaments by Catholic scholars transmits the best of modern scholarship to a wide audience.

Brown, Raymond E. *Biblical Exegesis and Church Doctrine.* New York/ Mahwah, NJ: Paulist Press, 1985. In a series of essays Brown shows that Catholic New Testament exegesis is centrist (rather than liberal or conservative) and not destructive of Catholic doctrine.

_____. *Responses to 101 Questions on the Bible.* New York/Mahwah, NJ: Paulist, 1990. Written by one of the best Catholic biblical scholars of the twentieth century, this volume responds to frequently asked questions on such topics as fundamentalism, Mary, sacraments, and Peter.

Brown, Raymond E., Joseph A. Fitzmyer, and Roland E. Murphy, eds. *The New Jerome Biblical Commentary.* Englewood Cliffs, NJ: Prentice Hall, 1990. This one-volume commentary on the entire Bible includes topical articles on such topics as inspiration, hermeneutics, Jesus, and Pauline theology. Written by Catholic scholars, it is full of reliable and up-to-date information and is the best example of modern Catholic scholarship.

Collins, John J. and Dominic Crossan, eds. *The Biblical Heritage in Modern Catholic Scholarship.* Wilmington, DE: Glazier, 1986. The essays in this volume deal principally with the ecumenical reality of contemporary biblical scholarship and locate works by Catholics in this framework.

Fogarty, Gerald P. *American Catholic Biblical Scholarship: A History from the Early Republic to Vatican II.* San Francisco: Harper & Row, 1989. In tracing the story of American Catholic biblical scholarship from John Carroll to Vatican II, a distinguished church historian focuses on the struggles revolving around acceptance of a critical and historical approach to the Bible.

Harrington, Daniel J. *Interpreting the New Testament*. Rev. ed. Wilmington, DE: Glazier, 1988. This introduction to New Testament exegesis explains the methods described in the present essay and provides examples how they can be used in studying specific biblical texts. *Interpreting the Old Testament* (Wilmington, DE: Glazier, 1981) is similar in scope and content.

Megivern, James J., ed. *Bible Interpretation*. Official Catholic Teachings. Wilmington, NC: Consortium Books/McGrath Publishing Co., 1978. English translation of sixty-two documents, including Vatican II's Constitution on Divine Revelation, dealing with the place of the Bible in the Church.

Neuhaus, Richard John, ed. *Biblical Interpretation in Crisis. The Ratzinger Conference on Bible and Church*. Grand Rapids: Eerdmans, 1989. Presented at a conference in 1988, the four papers by Joseph Ratzinger, Raymond Brown, William Lazareth, and George Lindbeck explore the value of historical criticism and the role of the Bible in the Church.

Schneiders, Sandra M. *The Revelatory Text. Interpreting the New Testament as Sacred Scripture*. San Francisco: Harper Collins, 1991. This readable and comprehensive introduction to biblical hermeneutics takes account of new ways of reading texts and shows how some traditional theological topics take on fresh significance when set in a different context.

Senior, Donald, ed. *The Catholic Study Bible*. New York: Oxford University Press, 1990. The first part (almost 600 pages) consists of general and introductory articles, as well as reading guides for the various parts of the Bible. The second part provides the introductions, translations, and notes for the Old Testament according to the 1970 edition of the New American Bible and the thoroughly revised New Testament (1988).

ORTHODOX INTERPRETATION OF SCRIPTURE
by
Michael Prokurat

I. INTRODUCTION

The topic, the Bible and its interpretation in the Eastern Orthodox Church, is immense and will be investigated from a particular
perspective—from within the Tradition of the Orthodox church and
with an eye toward contemporary questions in the West relating to
"Bible."[7] We do not intend to review patristic interpretation, though
an appropriate option, but choose a broader historical overview of the
canon. Similarly, no evaluation of the historical-critical method in the
Orthodox church is contained herein, since it has been twice reviewed
in recent publications.[8] We further limit the topic by treating only the
Greek/Byzantine and Slavic/Russian churches, not out of a sense of
exclusivity but simply because they are most accessible to us liturgically,
historically, linguistically, sociologically, etc. A fuller treatment includ-

---

[7]   For many Orthodox Christians the Tradition of the Orthodox church
is ultimately inseparable from that of the West and the Whole of Christian history. Two of my teachers, the late Professor Georges Barrois
and Professor Victor R. Gold, both of whom are probably best known
for their contributions to the Oxford Annotated Revised Standard
Version (much of which was used again, with or without appropriate
accrediting, in the New Revised Standard Version), have contributed
greatly to the approach taken in this chapter. Although they would
both identify themselves first with the Western church—and each has a
formidable knowledge of the Eastern church as well—the approach itself
goes beyond geography.

[8]   Veselin Kesich, *The Gospel Image of Christ*, rev.ed., (Crestwood, NY:
St. Vladimir's Seminary Press, 1986) ch. 1.

ing all ethnic (or "national") Orthodox churches is desirable but not within the scope of this chapter.[9]

Our point of departure takes as a presupposition—which some might prefer to view as a hypothesis—that Scripture is, and ever has been, liturgical. Second, Orthodox Christians experience Scripture and its interpretation primarily as a liturgical celebration, other than in their private reading and study. On the first point, Scripture is liturgical, the statement is made in the strongest possible sense. To say it in simple terms, Scripture originated as the liturgy of the people of God. For the specialist, the *Sitz im Leben* of Scripture is the Temple liturgy of Jerusalem and the liturgy of the Church—along with their respective hierarchies.[10] In popular terms one might expand the long-used axiom that the Psalms are "the prayerbook" of the Temple and Church to include all the books of the Bible in this "prayerbook." In saying Scripture is liturgical, we do not mean to say merely that liturgy is scriptural; but moreover that what was originally liturgy became Scripture. Scripture had its emergence and continued existence in the liturgy, the liturgical life of the Temple and Church, the communal prayers of the people of God.

The second point, that Orthodox experience Scripture and its interpretation primarily as a liturgical celebration, is probably less

[9]   Due to the rarity of English language materials on the Bible in the Orthodox church, especially regarding questions on history and canon, incredible statements can be found even in recent scholarly publications. For example, Harry M. Orlinsky and Robert G. Brachter in *A History of Bible Translation and the North American Contribution* (Atlanta, GA: Scholars Press, 1991) 9, date the origins of the Slavic version of the Bible to the fifth century—400 years before any historian would claim that a Slavic alphabet was invented! Similarly, R. F. Collins in the *New Jerome Biblical Commentary* (Englewood Cliffs, NJ: Prentice Hall, 1990) 1043, makes the extraordinary statement that, "Since the nineteenth century, however, Russian Orthodox theologians generally have not accepted the deuterocanonical books." The claim is erroneous on grounds of liturgical and intelllectual history. [It should be noted that in other regards both A History of Bible Translation and the NJBC are accurate and recommended books.]

[10] This is not to say that exceptions cannot be found; for example, the imperial edict in Ezra does not lend itself to the same interpretation.

controversial but is offered in direct continuity with the first. As a straightforward description, Orthodox Christians—scholars, clergy, and laity—recognize the point as true.[11] Even so, one still might challenge the statement, to ask if this is as it should be. Given the first point and the self-understanding of the Orthodox as being the people of God par excellence when participating in divine service, the answer to the challenge question is yes.

There are many difficulties and dangers in a primarily liturgical understanding of the Word of God, of which two are discussed below. First, the liturgical celebration gives revelatory and historical, salvific events by God a mysteriological or "poetic-mythic" expression—and this is not easily understood. To the sympathetic, it looks as if the liturgy attempts to "recreate" events from the Bible by repeating the scriptural account, elaborated as a complete story. To the less than sympathetic, it looks as if the scriptural account has been expanded to such a degree in the liturgical celebration that it has gone far beyond available evidence and information, it is "out of bounds." To the Orthodox, the liturgical celebration is understood as *a participation in the event itself*, i.e., every Easter is a direct participation in the resurrection of Christ, every Eucharist is a participation in the one, historical Last Supper, etc. The liturgy is not meant to be a re-creation or repetition, nor is it meant to be a "rewrite" of the scriptural account, but a direct participation in the (scriptural) saving acts of God. For Russian philosophers and theologians early in this century, like N. Berdyaev and S. Bulgakov, the category "trans-historical"—a category capable of capturing hermeneutics and theology, or the larger meanings of history—includes those timeless events celebrated by the mysteriological or "poetic-mythic" liturgy.[12] This understanding of the living, liturgi-

---

[11] See Breck, *Power of the Word*, "Introduction," wherein this and the unity between "Word and Sacrament" are explained from an Orthodox perspective.

[12] For us in the West, schooled in logical positivism, such a category simply could not exist: Only a "primitive religion" would repeat a cyclical liturgical celebration within linear time. Fortunately, the explanations of religion and myth by Mircea Eliade (sensitive to his Orthodox background) and recent recognition of the inadequacy of *ratio rationalis* in describing the wholeness of the human being and society have both further sensitized us to the validity of liturgical expression.

cal Word is quite different from a commentary approach or confessional definition based upon a list of "The Books of Scripture"—though it need not be so.

The second difficulty in a liturgical understanding of Scripture is the historical question—what the text meant within its own context. Clearly, historical facticity is important. We agree with the apostle Paul that if Christ was not raised from the dead, then our faith is in vain. The Nicene-Constantinopolitan Creed also maintains a historical perspective, as does the general mainstream of the Judeo-Christian tradition. Still, it might be objected that such a liturgical understanding of Scripture better presents those trans-historical events than it does the historical. The objection largely misconstrues the character of what trans-historical means: historical facticity is not to be excluded, but included. Besides this, the Bible is the book of the people of God and not vice versa, and it was not written to satisfy modern preconceptions stemming from the philosophy of logical positivism.

II. ORAL AND WRITTEN

The first historical indications of the written biblical text that we have from within the Bible itself are the famous episodes of the finding of a book in the Temple (probably part of Deuteronomy) during Josiah's reign, and of the dictation by the prophet Jeremiah to Baruch in the sixth century B.C. The earliest scrolls and manuscripts of the biblical text (Qumran) are from a time much later than this, closer to the birth of Jesus; and due to the fragility of writing materials, it is unlikely that any significant quantity of earlier materials will be found, unless they are inscribed on metal or stone.

Our cultural preoccupation with the written text should not obscure our vision in seeing a reality that is foreign to us: The Bible in its own time was a product of and existed within oral culture(s). Even the written Torah or Pentateuch text, brought from Babylon by Ezra in the fifth century and ceremonially read (i.e., read aloud) in its entirety from a platform constructed near the Water Gate,[13] was accompanied by an oral translation and/or interpretation (Neh 8). Many examples point toward the primacy of the spoken word: "Hear, O Israel: The

---

[13]   The Water Gate is identified as the "east gate of the Temple" in 1 Esdras 9:38, which connects Ezra's reading with the Temple area or thereabouts.

LORD is our God, the LORD alone.... Recite them to your children and talk about them when you are at home and when you are away, when you lie down and when you rise" (Deut 6:4f.). For those needful of more examples, suffice it to say that scholars recognize that the verb "to read" in the ancient world primarily meant "to read aloud." Thus, we are obligated to do business with the fact that the Bible within its own time was not primarily experienced as a book or scroll but as the spoken and proclaimed word. What does this mean to us today and what difference does it make?

What does it mean? The first consequence of "orality" in this sense is that the words have a "living" aspect: They are especially "alive" when experienced and spoken; and they are entrusted to a community of faith, often termed the people of God. For Americans who belong to "liturgical churches," this should not be a difficult concept. The "holy words" are part of the communal expression of worship, then as now: "Assemble the people—men, women, and children, as well as the aliens residing in your towns—so that they may hear and learn to fear the LORD your God and to observe diligently all the words of this law..." (Deut 31:12f.). When codified these "holy words" (or Word of God) are understood as the "Book of the People."[14] For the Orthodox Christian all of these elements—the salvific events, the experience of the community of people of God, and the liturgical expression of this experience (the "holy words") in proclamation and preaching—are constitutive to the interpretation of Scripture. For example, the deliverance from Egypt, the formation of the people delivered, as well as the Song of Miriam celebrating the events, are all part of Tradition—even including the liturgical celebration of the event through the ages and today on Pascha (Easter). The original oral tradition is intrinsically connected to present-day liturgical usage, through the mediation of Holy Scripture and its interpretation, all a part of a living, uninterrupted continuum.

What difference does it make? A normative way one may participate in Holy Tradition, especially the saving acts of God, is in the

---

[14]   Contrast this understanding with the accurate Moslem self-identification, "People of the Book," since the Koran was primarily a literary work. Christians ignorant of Islam and the history of the people of God sometimes identify themselves as the "People of the Book"—an unfortunate misrepresentation.

liturgy, mediated by Scripture; therefore, Scripture and preaching have a sacramental quality in the broader sense of the word. The Bible is not so much history, literature, or theology in the abstract, as it is the liturgical book of the Church. When we read our privately owned English-language Bibles in our homes, it is easy to forget that that literary milestone, the King James Version, was actually a translation from Byzantine liturgical texts. The codices from which modern English printed texts are translated might best be described as the liturgical books of the Church.

Why is the oral—and the liturgical—aspect of the Bible so difficult for us to grasp? First of all, it is because all modern Western cultures are "written" (and possibly "video" and "computer") before they are "oral." As Fr. A. Schmemann was fond of pointing out, there are more words printed every week in the Sunday edition of the New York Times than there are in the whole of the New Testament. What we have elsewhere called the "post-Gutenbergian" Bible—an individually affordable printed collection of all the books from Genesis to Revelation bound under one cover—has been the norm for so many centuries (in a culture focused on the individual) that we have forgotten how exceptional and rare a production, in historical terms, a private copy of the Bible is. Since individuals read the post-Gutenbergian Bible privately at will, and frequently devoid of community context, they risk being insensitive to the communal *proclamation* of the Word. Even the classical memorization of biblical passages has become individualized rather than community-focused in our American culture. The quest for individual salvation has eclipsed the reality that God usually saves the people of God first, and then saves individuals by incorporating them into his people. Private readings and interpretations—which have their place in Tradition too—have all but supplanted liturgical proclamation and interpretation.

Second, it is difficult to grasp the oral and liturgical character of the Word of God because even the names we use prejudice us in advance. The word "scripture" comes from the Latin *scriptum* and indicates something written. Similarly, the word "Bible" comes from the plural Greek word *biblia* (related to Byblos) and connotes books or a collection of books. As a result, the primary English terms we use for the Word of God both have to do with written books. Other cultures (e.g., Greek and Russian) do not always follow suit with this usage. This observation is not made with the intent of changing the English language terminology, but rather with the aim of shedding some light on our own American cultural predilections—one of the most difficult tasks of exegesis.

III. HEBREW AND GREEK

The history of the Hebrew books and language from the Babylonian Exile down through the Greek and Roman periods is a complex and shadowy one, about which scholars continue to debate—nor is it our purpose to broach all these questions. A few general observations should suffice. A consensus exists among scholars that the sixth century B.C., and more especially the time and place of the Babylonian Exile, was the matrix from which the Torah and most of the prophetic books emerged in their final written form.[15] The reasons for this had to do largely with the cessation of social institutions, liturgy, and the crises of the exiled community.

Primary social institutions for the small, pre-exilic Judahite state included the monarchy and the Jerusalem Temple, both of which became moribund during the Exile. With the end of the Temple came also the demise of its liturgy and liturgical interpretation, i.e., prophecy, all part of the fabric of life for centuries before the invaders. The cessation of the Temple liturgy, defeat by a foreign power (and god!), and the temptations of cosmopolitan Babylonian life created a well-recognized religious crisis of great depth. Among the memorable responses to this crisis—apocalypticism, a hope for return, the "Second Isaiah," etc.—were the codification of the Hebrew books and, quite possibly, the continuation of the liturgy in Babylon (without sacrifice) in a setting which eventually became the synagogue.

Even after the (partial) return of the Jews from Babylon in 539 B.C. and following, the work done there (Babylon) on what is now considered Scripture maintained a certain primacy. The Babylonian Jewish community was not only wealthier and more powerful than the Jerusalem community, but it had learned to transport physically the liturgy and its books, both of which expressed the identity of the people of God. Sacrifice remained the sole prerogative of the revivified Jerusalem community in the rebuilt Temple, a fact made plain by the

---

15 A more radical position, e.g., van Seter's and others, holds that most of these books were not only redacted, but moreover created, during the Exile. We find this position tendentious.

Aramaic correspondence between the Jerusalem Temple community and the Jewish communities at Elephantine in Egypt and in Babylon; but only the temple and the priesthood would survive as institutions in Jerusalem, while the monarchy and prophecy became silent—virtually non-extant.[16]

The intellectual precedence of the Babylonian Jews is illustrated in Ezra's return and in the liturgical reading of the books of the Torah or Pentateuch. Whatever the degree of Hebrew comprehension, when Ezra read the Torah in Hebrew, it was necessary for the Levites (or Ezra himself) to explain the incomprehensible words to his listeners (Neh 8) in Jerusalem. Ezra's "Bible" (Torah) was a manifestation of a religious and political alliance between Jerusalem and Babylon; and it was the liturgical book of the places where the hopes for liturgy had never ceased, where the priesthood was authoritatively represented. These constituted Ezra's claims to authority, along with the power of Persian support.

Not everyone was to accept Ezra's authority—or his "Bible"—and the exclusivistic authenticity he claimed for it. On one hand, by the first century B.C. the Samaritans would codify their own scriptures and give precedence to the Shechemite tradition over the Jerusalemite, preserving a text in Hebrew with some different spellings, but substantially the same as the Hebrew of the later Masoretes. Historical questions relating to the Samaritans and the Samaritan Pentateuch are appropriate to an investigation of the history of the Bible in the Persian, Hellenistic, and Roman periods, but are complex.[17] On the other hand, the Jewish colonies in Egypt appear to have an uninterrupted presence in that country from the time of the Exile (Jeremiah, Elephantine community, etc.) through the Roman destruction of Alexandria in the early second century A.D. Although we do not know as much as we might like about their liturgical practices and scriptures, the fact that they seemed to appeal to Jerusalem from time to time, and Jerusalem ac-

---

[16]   Michael Prokurat, *Haggai and Zechariah 1-8: A Form Critical Analysis* (University Microfilms International: *Dissertaion Abstracts International*, 4912A, June 15, 1989) 121f., 173f., 360f.

[17]   This is largely due to a terminological difficulty: All people living in the region of Samaria throughout the three periods are not to be identified as Samaritan religious sectarians who advanced Mt. Gerizim as a rival to Mt. Zion.

cused them of heterodoxy, would lead one to doubt their full compliance with Jerusalem liturgical and religious policy. (Indeed, when Alexandria became a leading city of the Mediterranean, the Jews there might have entertained an attitude of cosmopolitan superiority over their "suburban" neighbors in Jerusalem.) In this fluid context translations were made into Greek and Aramaic.

A commonly voiced opinion regarding the Hebrew and Greek Bibles, especially regarding the books of the First Covenant (i.e., Old Testament), was and is that the Hebrew Bible was the Jewish Bible, while the Greek was that of the Church. This rather simple view is at best misleading, if not one to be entirely rejected. A better description might be that the Hebrew and Greek Scriptures were both legitimate synagogue traditions, and the Church adopted the tradition of the Greek speaking synagogues—although even as late as the fourth century with St. Gregory Nazianzen (leader of the Second Ecumenical Council) and his contemporary, St. Jerome, we find some Christians expressing a preference for the Hebrew canon or listing of books.

Historical items that alert us to a parity claimed for the two contemporary traditions are the Letter of Aristeas (ca. 100 B.C.), referring to the Greek translation of the Hebrew, and Ben Sirach or Ecclesiasticus. The Letter of Aristeas resorts to exaggerated means to convince subsequent generations that the Jewish translators were not only qualified and working under Egyptian imperial tutelage, but that their product was created by a fantastic unanimity. Ben Sirach's grandson in the Prologue to his grandfather's work finds it necessary to warn the reader that the Greek does not always translate the exact sense of the Hebrew—an explanation necessary because many people assumed it did. Nevertheless, translational difficulties did not prevent him from presenting the Greek of his grandfather's work "for those living abroad who wished to gain learning, being prepared in character to live according to the Law." If the above interpretation of the evidence is insufficient to illustrate the parity claimed for the Greek translation with the Hebrew original, one could add the witnesses of the New Testament writers, and to that the voices of Philo of Alexandria and Flavius Josephus. Greek was here to stay.

At the same time as Ben Sirach translated writings from Hebrew to Greek (and possibly before), others translated biblical books, including the Pentateuch, from Hebrew into Aramaic. Known primarily from the medieval era as the Aramaic Targums (Targumim), some of these works originated even before the time of the Talmud and the classical rabbis. Several documents from Qumran testify to the early pre-Christian date of Aramaic translation efforts. Also, gospel quotes of Jesus' words on the cross are an Aramaic equivalent to a Hebrew psalm verse. Although the Targums have a long history of transmission, developing through the Byzantine period and beyond, the general phenomenon represents a good parallel to the translations from Hebrew to Greek and the widespread interest in the translation and interpretation of the Hebrew text in the ancient world through late antiquity.

The political unity of the ancient world achieved by Alexander and again by the Romans gave Greek an unprecedented ecumenical status among languages. One could say that Roman military might, Greek culture and language, and Jewish religion fascinated the world for centuries; and the Greek language was claimed by the ancients to have superiority over the Hebrew on purely linguistic grounds: spelling in Greek was more exact than the unpointed Hebrew text; and verb tenses and forms in Greek were more specific than their Hebrew counterparts, not to mention the accessibility of Greek to a worldwide population.

The translation of the Hebrew books into Greek accomplished an unanticipated equivocation of cultural structures between the Semitic and Greek worlds, the curious results of which we live with today. That is to say, the "transcultural" identification of Torah with Law, the Former Prophets with History, Covenant with Will or Testament, etc.—however necessary and inevitable from the translators' point of view—have given difficulty to readers and scholars from medieval times until the present. For example, it is generally acknowledged that the Hebrew word "torah" in most contexts is better understood as "instruction" or "teaching"; when given the sense of Roman (or American) "law," it becomes something different. Again, when the Torah and Former Prophets were entitled "writings and history" in the Septuagint, in medieval times they soon became "all the history of the universe," even though that meaning was never implied by the Hebrew titles— nor did scholars through late antiquity force that understanding on them.

Finally, and probably most significantly, "covenant" was translated with "testament"—a possible result of the lack of international (or suzerainty) covenants, made obsolete in the Hellenic and Roman periods by the conquests of Alexander and Rome. As theologians have been learning throughout the twentieth century, covenant not only had a millennium's worth of history behind it *at the time of the Babylonian Exile*, but represented a significant, living relationship between a king and vassal—much more than a death bequest. Both Jesus and Paul doubtless had "*berith*" or "covenant" on their lips and in their minds for the "words of institution" and at other times, but the Greek translation does not readily convey it to us.

For contemporary questions regarding Hebrew and Greek Bibles in which Orthodox participate, a few remarks are in order. Since both the Greek and Russian churches use the Lucianic Septuagint, there is a tendency among the faithful to romanticize the unanimity of the liturgical witness and beauty of language, depicting the history of the Greek Scriptures as devoid of controversy and independent of the Hebrew. History reveals flaws in this attitude. For example, during the fourth century (considered by some Orthodox to be a theological apogee) there were three different Septuagints in use in the major Christian centers of the eastern Mediterranean: (1) The churches in Antioch and Constantinople used the Lucianic recension. (2) Caesarea in Palestine utilized a translation by Origen that was updated by Pamphilus and Eusebius. (3) Alexandria had a third recension by a certain Hesychius about which little else is known. The Constantinopolitan practice, based on a translation done by the Presbyter Lucian (who preferred Attic forms) in that same century, finally won out.

Another example of the Hebrew-Greek issue can be found in the major works of that instructor of the Cappadocian Fathers, Origen. Probably due to his extensive influence in matters christological, these concerns eclipsed his primary effort and that of the entire Alexandrian School: Scripture. It should be remembered that his greatest research effort was a comparison of the Hebrew original, occupying the first column of his Scripture listings, with the various Greek renderings; and his work may be cited as a direct predecessor to the Septuagint translation work of the fourth century, mentioned above. The point here is that Origen began with the Hebrew original, transliterated it into Greek, and proceeded to list the various Greek translations as compared to the Hebrew. For Origen, the Hebrew text was the controlling factor to which the Greek had to be compared.

Today, the relationships between the various Hebrew and Greek textual traditions have to be taken very seriously, as seriously as Origen took them, especially in regard to the many new resources and tools we now have at our disposal. This was illustrated in the nineteenth century by Patriarch Philaret of Moscow who oversaw the Russian Bible translation (see below), which is now published and used by the Russian church. In addition, one of the greatest resources illuminating the relationship between the Hebrew and Greek textual traditions has been given us within this century by the discoveries at Qumran. Qumran has proved that both the Hebrew Masoretic text and the Greek Septuagint are faithful and credible witnesses to the ancient traditions and manuscripts. In many ways, certainly because of the discovery and availability of new information, we are presently in a position to do work with Scripture that was impossible even a half century ago.

IV. THE LANGUAGE OF THE COUNCILS

All ("Chalcedonian") Orthodox churches look to the Seven Ecumenical Councils, and related local councils, as a definitive manifestation of Holy Tradition, as a statement of faith over time, as a norm of "orthopraxy," etc.; and the traditions and decisions of these Councils are very much alive today, from the Nicene-Constantinopolitan Creed to iconography. Issues relating to Scripture existed at each of the seven, though we shall limit our investigation to some general considerations, particularly the topic of the canon or list of books to be read—both in church and otherwise.

Even though history has not given us the minutes of the First Council in A.D. 325, we do know from other writings and subsequent councils that questions about Scripture were on the agenda. The primary theological debate over Scripture at the First Council had to do with its use within a common creed, a creed with roots in Caesarea, later called the Nicene Creed. One group insisted that a creed could only use words found in Scripture, while the prevailing consensus claimed that the words of Scripture do not exhaust divine revelation and human experience; and the history of intellect and passage of time had raised new questions which would best be answered by "contemporary language." Gnosticism and Arianism had created a crisis that only the Greek word "homoousios" or "consubstantial"—a nonbiblical word—could address. The same group maintained that the description of Jesus Christ as "homoousios" or "of one essence with the Father" was in fact "Biblical," though the word itself does not appear in the Bible. Briefly, they argued that the word was not a *new* definition or new revelation of

God but merely a restatement of Holy Tradition using contemporary (fourth-century) language; paraphrasing St. Paul in 1 Corinthians 11 and 15, what has been received is being passed on.

St. Athanasius of Alexandria, recognized as a motivating theological force at Nicaea and author of the "Life of St. Anthony," issued a paschal encyclical (Easter letter A.D. 369) listing the books to be read in his diocesan churches. Although the first definitive listing of books came from a hierarch as an edict, it was understood to be representative of church practice handed down from the Apostles—the "Canon of Truth." This was the first extant document to list the twenty-nine books of the New Testament which we recognize today. Further, the list had no efficacy outside Athanasius's diocese but was given special recognition because of his status within the church and Alexandria's position as a leading city of the Empire. We proceed to an examination of select canons from the conciliar period.

Apostolic Canon #85: This earliest canonical reference to a list of the books of Scripture is difficult to date, just as any one of the Apostolic Canons is difficult to date individually; but we have discovered that the body of eighty-five canons was compiled by the first half of the fourth century, probably shortly after the First Ecumenical Council. It is unnecessary to assert that Canon #85 was written by an apostle, but it has always been given "apostolic authority" within the Orthodox church (even before the Council of Trullo). We know that the Apostolic Canons do represent the earliest canon law of the Church and probably originate before the year 300. It is traditional to ascribe the greatest authority to this particular canon when examining all those ecclesiastical rules that pertain to a determination of the books of Scripture.

"Let the following books be counted venerable and sacred by all of you...." Such a forceful beginning clause clearly shows the high status of Scripture. The first group which the canon lists are those books of the First Covenant (Old Testament). Among these are contained many deuterocanonical books, i.e., Wisdom of Solomon, three Books of Maccabees, etc. Besides these the Church recommends to teach the young people Ecclesiasticus (Wisdom of Sirach). With this admonition the Church recognizes the value of a certain book, although not one necessarily recommended for liturgical usage. Such a position is an important attitude to observe: a nonliturgical book has a marked, recognized value.

The second list in the canon enumerates books of the New Testament. In addition to the Gospels and Epistles one would expect, Revelation is most notably omitted, while two Epistles of Clement and the Constitutions of Clement are appended. The Constitutions are addressed to the bishops and are not to be read by all, "on account of the mystical things in them," probably referring to the *disciplina arcani*, i.e., reticence in revealing details of Christian mysteries (sacraments). With this brief advice we can sense a principle of discernment and discretion. Not everyone is able to read absolutely everything and understand it properly. Both Scripture and liturgy bear a certain "gnosis" that needs to be interpreted correctly.

The Metered Poems of St. Gregory the Theologian: Dating from the middle of the fourth century, this poem gives advice as to which are the "genuine books" of Scripture. It has been given the authority of a canon. St. Gregory remarks that many malignant books have been circulated and caution should be shown in choosing scriptural readings. He lists twenty-two books of the Old Testament. Those that he omits are Esther, 1 Esdras, and all the deuterocanonical books. This is the shortest Old Testament canon (accepted and approved) and is closest in content to the "Hebrew Bible." Of the books of the New Testament St. Gregory mentions twenty-six. He omits the Revelation. Of note, the apostle John is referred to as "the enterer of heaven"; and thus there seems to be an indirect reference to Revelation. It is interesting that Gregory has indicated a knowledge of Revelation and has not included it in his canon.

Iambics of St. Amphilocius, Bishop of Seleucus: Later in the fourth century Gregory's cousin, St. Amphilocius, wrote "the most true canon of the divinely given Scriptures." In the wording of this canon we find some helpful and revealing information: "We should know that not every book which is called Scripture is to be received as a safe guide. For some are tolerably sound and others are more than doubtful." Obviously, there must have been many different and variant books of Scripture disseminated, possibly those of the gnostic corpus, which were labeled undependable by the majority opinion. It is noteworthy that Amphilocius uses the terminology "tolerably sound" in referring to some of the books. It seems that there was a very fine line that divided those books which were acceptable, yet doubtful, from the other books that were unacceptable, but still worthy of consideration. Additionally, he enumerates the books as those "which the inspiration of God hath given." In the Old Testament canon he lists all of the protocanonical books but omits the deuterocanonical ones. At the end of this first list he continues, "to these some add Esther."

In his list of books of the New Testament canon all the usual ones are included except Revelation. The comment concerning the Revelation of John is that some accept it, "but by far the majority say it is spurious." It seems that Amphilocius considers it in the category of "very doubtful, but accepted by *economia.*" Such hazy distinctions and a willingness to make plausible concessions show that the Fathers of the Church used a methodology that was both flexible and open to considerations of rational discourse.

Synod of Laodicea, Canon #59: Dating from the second half of the fourth century, the text proper does not have to do directly with establishing a body of Scripture but rather with controlling the texts that are read in church: "No psalms composed by private individuals nor any uncanonical books may be read in church."

An established interpretation of this canon reveals that the rule approves only those hymns and antiphons which are sanctioned. All reading of nonsanctioned private compositions is prohibited. The canon is not meant to restrict hymns and readings solely to that of scriptural origin. The relevance this position has to our study is that the Church herself exercised authority to judge that which was to be read within her "ecclesia." She did not close the possibility of further expansion of the body of material read, but took the power to discern what that body would be. We well know that she later approved many hymns of private composition and incorporated them into the liturgical cycle.

Synod of Laodicea, Canon #60: The genuineness of this canon is vigorously questioned. Briefly, its text is a detailed list of those books that are to be included in the Scriptures. There are significant omissions of some of the more controversial books, i.e., Revelation, all the Books of Maccabees, Wisdom of Solomon. As a result of these important omissions and the questionable authorship of the text, many commentators ascribe little importance to it.

African Code, Canon #24: In this canon of the early fifth century we find a detailed list of the canonical Scriptures which the members of the African church "have received from our fathers to be read in the church." It is the most complete and lengthy compilation of books other than Apostolic Canon #85, and actually conforms the closest to the Bible printed today, with the deuterocanonical books (omitting 3

Maccabees and the Prayer of Manasseh) and all the books of the New Testament. This list differs from the Apostolic Canon in its omission of the Clementine writings and Ecclesiasticus and its inclusion of Revelation.

The wording of the introductory clause, "that besides the canonical Scriptures nothing be read in church under the name of divine Scripture," gives indication of problematic factors in the ecclesiastical situation. It is clear that other texts were read or sung besides the Scriptures. Of these the African council had no fear. Rather they were dealing with the problem of heretical or spurious books being read in the church with the authority, sanctity, and veneration that they accorded only to the divine Scriptures. Against these pseudepigraphic writings the Church of Africa wanted to protect its members.

Hippo (393), Canon #36: Briefly, this is the ancient epitome of Canon #24 of the African Code. Hippo, in addition to the above, allowed the readings of the "passions of the Martyrs" on the anniversaries of the martyrs' deaths. Possibly, nothing aside from Scriptures and the "passions" was read in the African church before the African Code, while antiphonal and nonscriptural compositions were sung rather than read. In any case, we can only speculate as to the reason that the "passions of the Martyrs" was dropped from liturgical use in the African church between A.D. 393 and 419.

Quinisext, Canon #2: At end of the seventh century the Council of Trullo (Quinisext) gave blanket approval to all canons previously recognized in the Church, including the bulk of the above canons. Specific mention is made of the Apostolic Canons in relation to a determination of a list of biblical books. Quinisext chose to omit the Constitutions of the Holy Apostles written by Clement because erroneous teachers had introduced heretical doctrines into the Constitutions, and they were rejected "so as the better to make sure of the edification and security of the most Christian flock."

As a result of this Quinisext canon, one is led to conclude that the approval of the canon of Scripture given was not specific, but general. This conclusion is true in part because the various canons cited conflict as to their content. Nevertheless, attention should focus on this second canon of Trullo, with its emphasis on Apostolic Canon #85. Whereas later canons are only mentioned by name, there are no less than ten lines of discussion and commentary on Apostolic Canon #85. Given the authority of apostolic authorship, it was also the first and most detailed commentary found in ecclesiastical law concerning the canon of Scripture. No set criticism existed at this time claiming that later canons superseded their predecessors; and in this case it might be argued that the opposite is true, the earliest canon was seen as the most authoritative. Therefore, we are left with the conclusion that Apostolic Canon #85 was accepted at Trullo as the principal canon of Scripture, though a "first among equals." (Other later canons at Trullo reflected on the character of individual books.)

In 787 the Seventh Ecumenical Council in its first canon *accepted all the canons of the Sixth Ecumenical and the Quinisext Councils.* As we have seen, the second canon of Quinisext gave blanket approval to many differing traditions concerning the content of the Bible, and this approval was confirmed by the Seventh Council. Where does that leave us when we attempt to describe the attitude toward the listing of biblical books at Quinisext and the Seventh Council? There seem to be three tenable possibilities (enumerated in an ascending order of preference):

1.   The fathers at these councils accepted Apostolic Canon #85 as having the greatest authority and omitted the Constitutions because they had been heretically corrupted. This comprised the content of the Bible they used.

2.   Either they did not consider the differences in the various canons of Scripture as important, or they saw them as constructive criticism of the value of the diverse books contained therein.

3.   They were heir to a liturgical cycle that determined the readings in the churches, and this cycle made the question of the canon of Scripture an "empty problem": *Lex orandi est lex credendi.* The several liturgical practices adequately and accurately represented the faith of the Church.

Based on the tradition of the Seven Ecumenical Councils, it is legitimate to assert that the Church has continually used discernment in her selection of scriptural readings. She has encouraged members to utilize discretion and understanding in their use of authorized and unauthorized books. Also, positive spiritual value can be ascribed to nonscriptural, apocryphal, or pseudepigraphic texts that are nonetheless beneficial to Christian readers—in spite of ecclesiastical prohibition of liturgical recitation.

V. LATIN

The glorious history of the translation of the Bible into Latin is well known from the writings of St. Jerome. As we shall see below, one of the first translations of the entire Bible into Church Slavic was made from a Latin edition shortly before the Reformation. The whole of this translation project from Latin to Slavic had a profound affect on Russian culture in the following centuries. During this time theological education in Russia was conducted exclusively in Latin, both spoken and written. Russian textbooks and theological treatises did not exist. In spite of the fact that Latin occupies a special place as the language of the Vulgate and as the medieval theological language of Europe, the focus of Orthodox attention on the Latin Bible lies elsewhere.

Orthodox commentary on the Latin of St. Augustine, especially in regard to his anthropology, spans over fifteen hundred years, from the time of his contemporaries (see Theodore of Mopsuestia and John Cassian) to the present.[18] The commentary is quite consistent, but is negatively critical; and it has gone relatively unheeded because it undermines Augustine's teaching on original sin—foundational to Western anthropology and soteriology, if not to Western culture as a whole. The attitude of Orthodox theologians toward Augustine and his pre-Vulgate Latin Bible (or toward his Trinitarian theology) probably appears curious to Westerners, since the Orthodox are happy to recognize the man's sanctity, learned achievements, profound insights, etc.; but they take exception to particular theological formulations, labeling them erroneous—for which they in turn are accused of being semi-Pelagian.

Reciprocally, the Orthodox are surprised at the complete acceptance of all of Augustine's theology by Western theologians. As Vladimir Lossky has pointed out, the reasons for this misunderstanding lie in the status accorded "Doctors of the Western Church" in medieval times, i.e., if one subscribes to all the teachings of a recognized doctor, one will be without theological error; and Augustine enjoys this status.

[18]   David Weaver, "From Paul to Augustine: Romans 5:12 in Early Christian Exegesis," *St. Vladimir's Theological Quarterly*, XXVII, 3 (1983) 187-206; XXIX, 2 (1985) 133-59; XXIX, 3, (1985) 231-57. Stanislas Lyonnet, S.J., "Les sens de ἐφ' ῷ en Rom. 5, 12 et le'exegese des Peres Grecs," *Biblica*, 36 (1955) 436-56 and "Le Péché Originel en Rom 5, 12," *Biblica*, 41 (1960) 325-55.

Not only does the East consider this medieval attitude to be uncritical from a scholarly point of view, but also outside of Christian Tradition: Doctrinal "infallibility" is a very specialized concept that is not attributed to individuals, but is most often used in historical retrospect to describe conciliar decisions of the whole Church.[19] Further, lest one get the impression that this approach is solely a critique of medieval Roman Catholic theology, the Orthodox see a similar attitude toward authority in the churches of the Reformation. For example, if not the writings of Augustine, then those of Luther, Calvin, or other of the Reformers are frequently accorded a de facto—if not dejure—"infallible status" by many Protestants today.

Augustine's anthropology, especially regarding creation, original sin, baptism, and grace, is an integrated system and is based to a large extent on his close exegesis of Romans 5:12. Unfortunately, the pre-Vulgate North African Latin Bible he used (and that Ambrosiaster used before him) mistranslated St. Paul[20] and read, "Sin came into the world, and death through sin, and so death spread to all men, through one man, *in whom* all men sinned (*in quo* omnes peccaverunt)." The Greek prepositional phrase should be translated, "by *which* (death) all men sinned." [However one translates the phrase, the question is the proper antecedent to the pronoun. Greek, like English, accepts the last recurring noun as the antecedent, which in this case is "death."] Augustine's Scripture told him that everyone sinned in Adam, ergo original sin. Paul actually said that death came into the world because of Adam's

---

[19]   Nevertheless, the East admits of no guarantees for conciliar doctrinal infallibility (which are contemporaneous with the council being held). Many councils were convened which proclaimed themselves "Ecumenical" and were not so recognized. That is to say, the classical question of authority is hadled quite differently in the East from the way it is handled in the West.

[20]   Remarkable, a translational ambiguity is maintained in English language Bibles at this point today as well when the render the Greek as "because."

sin, and resultingly all people sin because of their fear of death, something quite different from the above, and also more judicious for the rest of humanity.[21]

As J. Pelikan has shown,[22] Augustine expands this idea of original sin, following Ambrosiaster at first (whom Augustine quotes), then rooting it in procreation; but such a view of sin and procreation is dangerously close to—if not identical with—the standard Manichaean view Augustine held for nine years before his adult conversion to Christianity, and for which his contemporaries criticized him. Paul's view of the matter—we remember Paul was trained as a rabbi—had nothing to do with sexuality per se, original sin, or original guilt. It might better be characterized by 2 Baruch 54:15, 19: "For though Adam first sinned and brought untimely death upon all, yet of those who were born from him each one of them has prepared for his own soul torment to come, and again each one of them has chosen for himself glories to come.... Adam is therefore not the cause, save only of his own soul, but each of us has been the Adam of his own soul."

The gnostic doctrine Augustine read into his Latin Bible included not only the sexually transmitted sin and guilt of original sin, but also the doctrine of the "distorted human image," which rendered the image of God in human beings "destroyed."[23] This may be contrasted with a general insistence in the East on the "undistorted image of God"

---

[21]   How do the Orthodox understand Romans 5:12? Since Paul's thought can be schematized as typological parallelism in Romans 5:12-21, repeated in 6:15-23, and another in 1 Corinthians 15:40-49, there should be little doubt as to what he meant. For example, for type-prototype read: Adam-Christ, sin-grace, death-life, etc., all of which are causally connected and run parallel. Again, the essence of Romans 5:12-21 is summarized in 6:23, "For the wages of sin is death, but the free gift of God is eternal life in Christ Jesus our Lord." This typological parallelism, sometimes studied under the rubric of chiasm, compares favorably with the "descedning and ascending" pattern long recognized in Phillipians 2:5f., which is usually categorized as a pre-Pauline hymn.

[22]   See Jaroslav Pelikan, *The Emergence of the Catholic Tradition (100-600)*, Vol. I of the *The Christian Tradition* (Chicago: The University of Chicago Press, 1971) 299-301.

[23]   *Ibid.*

in men and women, wherein only the likeness needs to be recovered, while the image is latently preserved.[24] Nonetheless, Augustine put the "new" Christian doctrine to work with great results, but with a focus that further separated him from classical Pauline theology.

Augustine used the revised doctrine primarily as a foil against the Pelagians who claimed that baptism was unnecessary. His response was that baptism was absolutely necessary due to the human being's "destroyed nature" which was in need of baptism and grace. This almost metaphysical argument may be contrasted with Paul's emphasis on baptism as a return from idolatry and a false creaturely independence. Similarly, in dealing with the baptism of infants Augustine's focus is on deliverance from "original sin." For Paul baptism is certainly characterized as being for "remission of sins," but the majority of references deal with baptism "into Christ."[25] In both instances regarding baptism Augustine favors a metaphysical, problem-solving approach aimed at individual salvation, while Paul speaks primarily about an imitation of the death and resurrection of Christ, which addresses a sinful world, but more than anything, incorporates all members into a life in Christ and the Church. Ultimately, for Augustine this doctrine became the entire providential reasoning behind the incarnation: someone had to be born virginally, without original sin and with an undistorted nature, in order to return humanity to the same "sinless" (asexual?) state. This position is a far cry from Paul's interpretation of the road to Damascus episode, John's reporting of Jesus' first miracle at Cana, or Athanasius's *On the Incarnation*, all of whom understood God as self-revealing by nature, and not providentially constrained to respond to a difficulty caused by human sexual behavior.

---

[24] It should be sobering for theologians to recognize that what was originally a Heberew parallelism, "image and likeness," has been dissected, been given distinct meanings, been passed through a gnostic filter, been served up repeatedly during the Reformation, and is still an object of ongoing debate in Christian anthropology.

[25] From the available evidence it does not seem that infant baptism was an issue in Paul's time, since the baptism of households probably would have included all the dependent members, slaves, children, etc., just as the celebration of Passover in Jewish households would have been inclusive of all household members.

Although Jerome's Vulgate cleared up difficulties with differing Old Latin editions that circulated in Rome and North Africa, Augustine's (forgivable) eisegesis remains with us. Today, if one asks any Westerner what Adam and Eve's sin was, the answer "sex" is given unhesitatingly and unanimously—the gnostic myth remains, the Greek scriptural text notwithstanding. This attitude is not only a popular misconception, but functions at "high" theological levels: witness the recent New Revised Standard Version rendering of Psalm 51:5, "Indeed, I was born guilty, a sinner when my mother conceived me," incorporating Augustinian "original sin" and "original guilt" into one line (wherein the Revised Standard Version had been more careful). The Orthodox understand this form of Gnosticism to be not only misogynous, but misanthropic, denying a positive value to human sexuality—which is not denied in any biblical text.

VI. SLAVIC AND RUSSIAN

The traditional beginnings of the translation of the Bible into Slavic are with those fathers of Slavic literary culture, Cyril (+869), baptized Constantine, and his older brother Methodius (+884). Cyril, known as "Constantine the Philosopher" for his academic skills, and Methodius, who would later continue translation work with disciples in Bulgaria after his brother's death, were members of the Slavic-speaking community in Thessalonika, part of a "Slavic presence" there dating back at least to the sixth century A.D. The brothers were accomplished linguists, and Cyril remarkably so, mastering Greek, Slavic, Latin, Hebrew, and Syriac. They were both employed by the Byzantine Emperor Michael III and the great Patriarch Photius as emissaries to the Arabs and Khazars, and primarily as missionaries to Slavic-speaking lands on the Danube and in the Balkans. By the time Prince Rostislav of Moravia requested missionaries from Constantinople to teach his people their own language (862)—in order to foil German political ambitions—it is probable the brothers had already begun working on some type of alphabet.

The early history of the Slavic Bible is too complex to repeat in full, but some of the more notable points bear mentioning, many of which are historical ironies. The first quirk of history is that the Slavic alphabet attributed to Constantine-Cyril's inventiveness (Cyrillic) was probably created later by Methodius's disciples in Bulgaria in the last decade of the ninth century.[26] Many scholars now believe that Constantine-Cyril devised another alphabet, Glagolitic, which was utilized by the Moravians but soon fell into disuse; and his had not been the first attempt. Earlier in the same century two Byzantine emperors tried unsuccessfully to synthesize a Slavic alphabet; and the Franks translated a small liturgical selection of Christian texts from Latin into Slavic with the use of Latin letters.

A second irony is that the preliterary Slavic language had no theological or religious vocabulary, nor a vocabulary of philosophy or social institutions, which could serve as a basis for translation. Composite Greek words, like our English "theo-logy" and "tris-agion," became new Slavic words with identical composition from Greek roots. The influence of the Greek Bible was so formative in the development of the Slavic Bible over the next century, or rather of Slavic literary language in general, that the word count and word order often became the same in both Bibles. This was true to a surprising degree: When particles existed in Greek which had no Slavic counterpart, a particle was invented and inserted into the Slavic biblical text at the appropriate point! (Compare Aquila's Greek translation of Hebrew a little over one-half millennium earlier.) No other literary language, with the possible exception of Hebrew, was so profoundly influenced by the biblical text. The Slavic language became "literate" in conformity to the Greek Bible which gave it its vocabulary and syntax, as well as its theological orientation.

A third historical riddle begins with the Moravians, who originally requested Byzantine missionaries and received the help. The missionaries made use of the Slavic vernacular liturgically and in preaching, but the Moravians did not become the primary vehicle of the Byzantine-Slavic mission. This lot fell to Boris of Bulgaria who, within a few years of the original mission, accepted Christianity from Constantinople in order to be delivered from the Moravians! The Slavic

---

[26]   Roman Jakobson, "St. Constantine's Prologue to the Gospel," *St. Vladimir's Seminary Quarterly*, VII, 1 (1963) 14-19 and other titles in the same number. Special thanks to Dr. Thomas Klocek of DePaul University for an updated bibliography on the Ohrid literary school, including the following more accessible items: Radmila Ugrinova-Skalovska, "Clement of Ohrid and the Founding of the Ohrid Literary School," *Macedonian Review*, XVI, 3 (1986) 258-62. N.L. Tunitsii, *Sv. Kliment* (Tipografiia Sv. Tr. Sergiivoii Lavry, 1913) 224-60 [in Russian].

vernacular was successfully salvaged by the Bulgarians when they granted asylum to Methodius's circle of disciples, e.g., Clement of Ohrid (Ochrida) and others.

The fourth and last equivocation falls to the Byzantines. When Constantine-Cyril and Methodius first began to read the Bible and pray in Slavic, they were accused of heresy by the Latin Christians. The "three-languages heresy" was a belief that the Bible could only be read in one of the three languages inscribed on the cross of Jesus—Hebrew, Greek, or Latin. In spite of the Latin charge the brothers remained firm in their resolve to continue using Slavic, ostensibly defended by Constantinople. The Byzantine equivocation lies in the fact that not all the Greeks were convinced of the legitimacy of the use of Slavic: the Emperor thought that translation was a departure from tradition; Constantine-Cyril was afraid of an accusation of heresy from the Greeks when he prayed in Slavic; and indeed, the same recriminations reappeared with the arrival of Greek missionaries in Bulgaria within the century.[27] Although Constantinople theoretically acknowledged the theological validity of the use of other languages, in practice they displayed a bit of "Byzantine chauvinism."

As with the history of the translation of the Septuagint from Hebrew, so too the translation of the Lucianic recension and the New Testament from Greek into Slavic is clouded by half-truths. The popular version of the history says that the older Methodius and two of his disciples finished translating all the books of the Bible from Greek after the death of brother Cyril, that is between 869 and 884. This description is probably based on an oversimplification or the desire to have the sainted brothers finish the monumental task within their lifetimes. A decade or so later the exarch John of Bulgaria said that Cyril had translated the Gospel Book and Epistle Book, while Methodius had translated sixty other books from Greek into Slavic. Even if we employ a short canon, which neither the Greeks nor the Slavs ever did, the numbers cited are insufficient for a whole Bible of any type. The early nineteenth-century Russian historian Metropolitan Evgenii (Bolhovitinov) stated that a full translation was never made by the sainted brothers. In addition, since no complete manuscript of the Slavic Bible

---

[27]   Dimitri Obolensky, *The Byzantine Commonwealth: Eastern Europe 500-1453* (Crestwood, NY: St. Vladimir's Seminary Press, 1971) 202-03.

exists from the whole of the Kievan Period (X-XIII), we may doubt whether the entire translation was executed during this time.

Nonetheless, the Kievan Period was not devoid of those interested in the Bible, especially in consideration of the popular power of liturgy and the personal piety of the people of Kievan Rus'. Since the Old Testament enjoyed limited liturgical use, only the prescribed Old Testament lectionary was collected into one liturgical book, in practice rendering a complete collection unnecessary. For both liturgical and private use, the available biblical books circulated in smaller collected editions. The psalter was the most popular one, outpacing even the gospels, and was used not only as the "prayerbook of the Church" but also as the only reading primer. After the psalter and gospels came the prophets and wisdom literature, especially Sirach.[28] The *Palaea*, a "Reader's Digest version" of the "historical books" of the Old Testament dressed up with apocryphal legends, completed the list. G. Fedotov characterizes the era as follows:

"In Russia [Kievan Rus'] the notion of the Biblical canon, distinguishing strongly between the inspired Holy Scripture and the words of the fathers, never existed. All religious writings were called sacred and divine insofar as they were not heretical. The Russian people had a particular predilection for the apocrypha [i.e., non-Biblical rather than "deuterocanonical"] because of its fabulous content which appealed to their imagination.[29]

While reading was a virtue of the elite, and liturgy appealed to both elite and common, Holy Scripture and apocryphal works were rivaled in popularity only by translations of the lives of saints. These were followed in the manuscripts by sermons and patristic exegeses. Thus, three of the largest and most popular literary corpora of Kieven Rus' had Holy Scripture as their centerpiece.

After a hiatus in biblical translation effort of not a few hundred years, we resume our investigation in Novgorod at the end of the fifteenth century, having witnessed the passing of the entire Appanage Period (Mongols) and the fall of Constantinople (Turks); and we stand

---

[28]   George P. Fedotov, *The Russian Religious Mind*, Vol. I: *Kievan Christianity: The Tenth to the Thirteenth Century*, John Myendorff, ed. (Cambridge, MA: Harvard University Press, 1966) 42-43.

[29]   *Ibid.*, 43.

on the brink of the coalescence of the kingdom of Muscovite Rus', or Great Russia. At this time the so-called "Judaizer heresy" arose, a movement that included translations of biblical books only from the Hebrew. The "Judaizers" were led by Zechariah (Slavic: Skharia), who was probably a Crimean Karaite Jew; and he taught that Christ was a prophet, the messianic prophecies were unfulfilled and still awaited fulfillment, the Church is unnecessary, etc. Besides the Old Testament, the group translated Maimonides and Algazel as well as astrological books.[30] When two Novgorodian priests influenced by the movement transferred to Moscow, the "Judaizer heresy" became marginally influential in the capital.

The main opponent of the Judaizers was Joseph of Volok (Iosif Volotskii), an abbot of the Volokolamsk Monastery. He successfully pursued them until they were condemned by a church council (1504) and eradicated by Ivan III. Joseph is best known in Russian history as the successful spokesman for the "possessors," over against Nilus of Sora (Nil Sorskii) who led the "non-possessors," in what became a legitimate minority position theologically, though less so politically. Simply put, the possessors believed in extensive church holdings and close cooperation with secular authority in order to do God's work, while the non-possessors minimized church holdings and preferred a separation between church and state.

It is probably not coincidental that Scripture figured into Joseph's controversies with the non-possessors no less than it had with the Judaizers. The non-possessors, somewhat in anticipation of what would occur in the West later in the same century, "differentiated in the teaching of the Church among Holy Writ, tradition, and human custom, considering only Holy Writ—that is, God's commandments—as completely binding. The rest could be criticized and changed."[31] Although both Joseph and Nilus were canonized, Joseph's "establishment" position better accommodated the rising centralization of the Muscovite state, while some of Nilus's disciples were condemned as heretics.

---

[30]   Georges Florovsky, *Ways of Russian Theology*, Part I, Vol. V of *The Collected Works of Georges Florovsky*, Richard S. Haugh, ed., Robert L. Nichols, tr. (Belmont, MA: Nordland Publishing Company, 1979) 15.

[31]   Nicholas V. Riasanovsky, *A History of Russia*, 5th ed. (New York: Oxford University Press, 1993) 123.

In the midst of the Judaizer and non-possessor controversies, the first-known, complete Slavic Bible was compiled in Novgorod. The translation effort, which went beyond solely biblical texts, was stimulated by and responded to the above-mentioned movements under the authorization and protection of Archbishop Gennadius of Novgorod— and became known in Russian as Gennadius's Bible (1499 and following). Political and polemical considerations undermined the integrity of the effort from the very beginning.

Neither Hebrew, Greek, nor extant Slavic translations were employed as primary texts from which to translate. Only the Vulgate was used. This phenomenon is indicative of a general orientation of Russia toward the Occident after the fall of Constantinople.[32] The Vulgate was supplied by a Dominican, Friar Benjamin (Veniamin), whose appearance in Novgorod might not have been accidental. The section headings for Gennadius's Bible were co-opted from a recently published German edition. Russian evaluations of the translation through modern times have been negative and focus on the "incursionary presence" of Roman Catholic politics on Russian soil. Other Latin texts which produced a European resonance in Russia were also translated at Archbishop Gennadius's residence. These included pieces focusing on messianism in Scripture, polemics against Jews, and church-state debates on property. Like it or not, Latinate influence would dominate major sectors of Russian ecclesiastical life for centuries to come.[33]

After the appearance of the first printed Epistle Book ("The Apostle") in 1564, the first full text of the Slavic Bible was published in 1580 and again with emendations in 1581. It was known as the Ostrog Bible after its chief patron, Prince Constantine of Ostrog (Konstanin Ostrozhskii). The work appeared as a part of a larger private publishing effort among the Orthodox in Lithuania and Poland, which included liturgical books and religious pamphlets—translational rather than polemical works.

Although all the Ostrog publications served apologetic purposes, the inspiration for this serious translation project came from a greater vision of Slavo-Hellenic culture, common to the participants in the

---

32 European contacts and ideas were more exciting than a static Byzantium, and they occasionally tempted the Russians away from their own traditions.

33 Florovsky, *Ways*, Part I, Vol. V, 14-19.

"Ostrog Circle." Trained in Greek, Latin, and Slavic, members of the Ostrog Circle rooted their work in their own tradition, while participating in the trilingual "Greek school," which lasted only a few decades. The Prince's school seemed to be a response to the Jesuit-sponsored College of St. Athanasius founded in Rome during the same period to educate Slavs and Greeks in Uniate Catholicism; and indeed they responded strongly to Uniatism and the calendar reform of Pope Gregory XIII. Nonetheless, the most stunning accomplishment of the Ostrog Circle was their Bible; and the quality of its Slavic text favorably compared to contemporary translations in other languages, for example the Sixtus Clementine version of the Vulgate (1592).[34] In evaluating the translation, Fr. G. Florovsky writes, "The Ostrog Bible, as such, remains a landmark in Slavonic Biblical history. It abides also as a magnificent achievement in itself, a monument of scholarship, literature, and theology." The members of the short-lived Circle were exceptional for their time and place, and many went on to other tasks of history-making significance.

Before leaving the Ostrog Circle, let us look briefly at their methodology. Employing classical Church Slavic, they attempted to follow the Greek textual tradition using every available critical resource. Starting first with Gennadius's Bible, other Greek and Slavic manuscripts were obtained with difficulty from Constantinople and monastic centers; but the manuscripts were disappointingly poor. After these, they consulted the (Masoretic) Hebrew text, the Vulgate, and recent Czech and Polish versions; and finally they checked their results against the Aldine Septuagint (Venice, 1518) and the Complutensian Polyglot (Spain, 1522) which contained parallel columns of Hebrew, Aramaic, Greek, and Latin Old Testaments, as well as Greek and Latin New Testaments. All subsequent editions of Church Slavic Bibles have been dependent on the text of the Ostrog Bible.[35] Clearly, anyone claiming an autonomy for the Slavic Bible exclusive of the Hebrew text or of Western scholarship knows neither this Bible nor its history.

As Prince Constantine of Ostrog went on to become an ecumenist of sorts, so too another of his Circle, Cyril Lukaris (1572-1638), went on to become the ecumenically minded Patriarch of Alexandria, and

[34] *Ibid.*, 42-45.

[35] *Ibid.*, 45.

later Patriarch of Constantinople.[36] Aside from his highly political relationship with the Church of Rome and the Turks, Cyril is best known
for his Calvinist *Confession* (statement of religious belief), published at
Geneva in 1629 and written in Latin six years earlier. Cyril was possibly the most important intellectual figure in the Eastern church at the
time, though doomed to tragic political and ecclesiastical circumstances;
and his *Confession* was condemned by no less than six local church
councils before the end of the seventeenth century.[37] With the repudia-
tions of Cyril's Calvinist statement of faith came a tacit, negative attitude
from the condemning hierarchy toward an enlightened use of the Bible
by the faithful. The reaction sometimes took on an aspect characteristic of contemporary, seventeenth-century Roman Catholic polemics.

Let us briefly summarize some of Cyril's actions pertinent to our
topic and the reactions he elicited.[38] In "Question III" of the *Confession*
Cyril lists the canon of Scripture as that of the Synod of Laodicea (see
the suspicious Canon #60 above); but he proceeds to change it to correspond exactly to the Calvinist canon, invoking the concept of
"apocrypha" for remaining books, and asserts that this had always been
the canonical reckoning of the Orthodox church! This particular de-
ception was uncovered at the Synod at Jassy in Moldavia (1642), the
second such synod condemning the *Confession*. The first local council
in Constantinople against Cyril's statement (1638) focused more on a
critique of Chapter II, wherein he claimed Scripture to be of higher
authority than the Church. Cyril argued that the Church was liable to
err, whereas Scripture was not. Certainly Cyril himself was liable of
error, as proved at the Synod of Jerusalem (1672). This local council
took pains to research his sermons and illustrate that he consistently
contradicted himself, referencing "apocryphal" books as authoritative

---

36 See Timothy Ware, *The Orthodox Church*, rev. ed. (Harmondsworth,
England: Penguin Books Ltd., 1993) 96-97.

37 See Dositheus, *The Acts and Decrees of The Synod of Jerusalem*, J.N. W.
B. Robertson, tr. (New York: AMS Press, 1969) for a point-by-point
response.

38 The Lukaris episode has never been fully investigated from the perspective of the history of the Bible in the Orthodox Church, probably due
to a preoccupation with the more immediate and prevalent doctrinal
and political issues.

Scripture and countermanding the doctrinal content of the *Confession*. In general the opposed synods were concerned with protecting the integrity of the teaching of the Church and the church fathers, as well as the listing of the books; and historically they were considered justified and consistent in their actions against the brilliant Patriarch.

In retrospect the difficulty with the Lukaris episode and the Bible seems to lie in other ad hominem condemnations, those designed solely to denounce the man and his nefarious teachings. But *not everything* Cyril taught was wrong, though it seems to have been subsequently treated as if it were. For example, in the *Confession* Question I reads: "Ought the sacred Scriptures to be read in the common language by all Christians?" Cyril answers, "All faithful Christians ought to know, believe, and confess, what is in the sacred Scriptures," which, with almost all the rest of the answer, is perfectly "Orthodox." Unfortunately, at one point he claims, "For neither can we learn from any other source than from the sacred Scriptures," which is insensitive to Orthodox pneumatology, ecclesiology, and Tradition in general.

The easily remembered "no" answer given the same question by Patriarch Dositheus at the Synod of Jerusalem (1672) is misleading for two reasons. First, his answer that Scripture ought not be read in the common language is insupportable from Tradition and is cited without precedent. Both the Synod of Constantinople (1638) and the Synod in Moldavia (1642) ignored it completely. Dositheus's canonical formulation—"to read some parts of the Scriptures, and especially of the Old (Testament), is forbidden for the aforesaid reasons and others of like sort"—requires a clear canonical precedent which is not, or rather cannot be, provided. Second, his answer is so highly qualified and nuanced that it appears that the fashioners of this response simply wanted to answer "no" when Lukaris answered "yes."

Dositheus uses a similar technique in answering Cyril's Question II ("Are the Scriptures plain to Christians who read them?"), which question is ignored by the local councils of Constantinople and Jassy. Cyril gives a qualified "yes" to the question and remains within the Tradition. Dositheus seems to change the question to read "all Christians"[39] and responds with a qualified "no." At this point the quantitative difference in their answers might be characterized by Cyril's glass being "half-full" while Dositheus's is "half-empty." Nevertheless, Dositheus

---

[39]   Dositheus, *Acts and Decrees*, 153.

pushes the point to conclude, "it is not necessary, but rather impossible, that all should know what the Holy Spirit manifests to those alone who are exercised in wisdom and holiness." Subsequent to the seventeenth century Dositheus's council has been given authoritative status, while Cyril and his *Confession* have been consistently condemned. One cannot help but think that in the particulars above, Dositheus's Orthodoxy was not any more reliable than Cyril's, and in some points less so.

In Russia the nineteenth century brought with it an avid interest in the Hebrew text of the Bible, especially among theologians, but also among members of the newly formed Russian Bible Society. Translations from Hebrew into Russian (instead of Church Slavic) drew mixed reactions from the hierarchy and from society at large for about fifty years, until the last quarter of the century. Notable figures produced personal translations: Makarii Glukharev (1792-1847), a seminary professor and Siberian missionary, translated Job (1837) and Isaiah (1839) from Hebrew as a testimony to his opinion that a Russian translation should be made from Hebrew; but he was officially reprimanded for his efforts toward that end. Archpriest Gerasim Pavskii (1787-1863), an eminent professor and Hebraist in St. Petersburg, court chaplain and tutor to the imperial family, produced a personal translation of the Old Testament which his students circulated clandestinely until all copies were confiscated in an investigation in 1842. Although Glukharev's and Pavskii's translations were eventually published in the mid-1860s, the Hebrew versus Greek debate continued—to an impasse for some who would admit only one tradition (e.g., P. I. Gorskii-Platonov accepted only the Masoretic Text, F. Govorov only the Septuagint)[40]; but for most scholars and churchmen of the last decades of the nineteenth century, the complex relationship between the Hebrew and Greek texts was not only acknowledged but researched in critical literature on a book-by-book basis.[41]

---

[40] Georges Florovsky, *Ways of Russian Theology*, Part II, Vol. VI of *The Collected Works of Georges Florovsky*, Richard S. Haugh, ed., Robert L. Nichols, tr. (Belmont, MA: Nordland Publishing Company, 1979) 348-49.

[41] *Ibid.* See the listing of major individual translations in endnotes 40-54, as well as on pages 124-28.

Organization and execution of the great Bible translation project of nineteenth-century Russia can be credited to only one individual, Metropolitan Philaret (Drozdov) of Moscow. In 1856 he personally urged the Holy Synod to undertake a new translation which would provide "the Orthodox people with the means to read Holy Scripture for instruction in the home and with the easiest possible comprehension."[42] An earlier translation had been completed and published in segments: the Gospels in 1819, the entire New Testament in 1820, the Psalter in 1822, and the rest of the Old Testament in 1825. Tragically, the completed work did not fare any better than its sponsors, A. Golitsyn and the Bible Society, whose activities were curtailed in 1825. With the printing complete, the work was not only suppressed, but completely destroyed.[43]

In the early phase of the project (1816-1825) Philaret had set forth guidelines for translation which were also used in the second half of the century. The translation was made from the Masoretic Hebrew as the basic text, and then from the Greek when it was the original language, giving both preference over extant Slavic translations. Literary form was analyzed and maintained: "The spirit of a passage must be painstakingly observed, so that conversation will be rendered in a colloquial style, narration in a narrative style, and so forth." He ranked the priorities of translation as accuracy first, clarity second,[44] and literary purity

---

[42] The project had originated forty years earlier when Tsar Alexander I (1801-1825) charged his friend A. N. Golitsyn, the head of numerous government religious and educational posts and the president of the newly formed Russian Bible Society, with complete responsibility in words similar to the preceeding ones. Although the Holy Synod was not involved at all—and it was assumed Church Slavic would continue to be used liturgically—the actual translation project was supervised by the able dean of the St. Petersburg Academy, Archimandrite Philaret, the future Metropolitan of Moscow.

[43] For particulars on the episode and the ill-fated Bible Society, see Florovsky, *Ways*, Part I, Vol. V, 181-201.

[44] One might see in at least the first two items, curiously juxtaposed, the heir of the slavish word-for-word translation from Greek to Church Slavic completed a millennium earlier, now canonized and taken as normative. This might be the reason that the vocabulary and syntax of the Russian Bible is not readily comprehensible to Russians.

third.[45] Philaret also gave directives regarding style; for example, "Holy Scripture derives its majesty from the power, not the glitter, of its words."[46]

As one might surmise, Philaret's guidelines for translation opened new questions which Russian society in the 1820s could not tolerate. The questions were difficult, legitimate, and could only be addressed through public discussion—which would not occur until later in the century. For example, for people who were troubled by the divergences of the Russian from the Slavic, especially in regard to preference given the Hebrew, explanation had to be made to pacify those unfamiliar with ancient languages. Another example, clear from the history already reviewed, is that the Slavic Bible itself could not be equated with the Septuagint, as everyone had supposed. It was composite and did not correspond in every respect to the Greek. Finally, as mentioned above, even the Hebrew and Greek texts enjoy a complex relationship which needs to be understood on a case-by-case basis.

Although Philaret's purpose appears to us clear and commendable, his efforts were opposed by some colleagues, notably Metropolitan Philaret (Amfiteatrov) of Kiev and the new Ober-Procurator of the Ministry of Religious Affairs, Count A. P. Tolstoi. Opposition stemmed from bad experiences with translators and the Russian Bible Society earlier in the century, as well as from an inbred hierarchical conservatism. The project had been successfully opposed in 1824 and 1842; and when it was proposed again in 1856, many reasons against it were articulated: There was a mistrust of the Hebrew Bible which was [falsely] described as "unknown in the Church." Earlier in the century the translations from Hebrew by Pavskii and Makarii caused heated controversy. Reference was made to the Greek church which did not allow translations into vernacular Greek.[47] The Russian language was accused of being less expressive than Church Slavic, and besides, the other liturgi-

[45]   Florovsky, *Ways*, Part I, Vol. V, 190.

[46]   *Ibid.*

[47]   Translation of the Bible into modern Greek was first blessed in 1808 by Patriarch Cyril VI of Constantinople; but it was subsequently resisted until the present decade, wherein the new translation sparked a hot debate.

cal books had not been translated, and so on.[48] In addition only Church Slavic translations were used liturgically (which remained the case throughout the Soviet Period).[49]

To the credit of midcentury Russian scholarship—and of Philaret's Job-like perseverance—the monumental Bible project was completed under the auspices of the Holy Synod and under the Metropolitan's watchful eye. The Gospel Book was published in 1860, the complete New Testament in 1862, and fascicles of the Old Testament began to appear in 1868. The complete edition appeared in 1875. All subsequent synodal editions built upon this one; and revisions were handled by the (now familiar) technique of citing the correction in the footnote and moving it into the text in the following printing. New editions were revised and republished until the decade before the Russian Revolution. When the Soviets published 500,000 Bibles to commemorate the millennium of Christianity in Rus' in 1988, they republished the last prerevolutionary revision of Philaret's Bible. This last fact probably best illustrates how biblical scholarship was forced to a standstill during the Soviet Period.

In the closing decades of the nineteenth century and the first of the twentieth one can recognize common elements in biblical studies in European Russia and in continental Europe. Although New Testament scholarship in Russia was less ardently pursued than Old, one finds many of the same learned writings and cultural fascinations as one finds in Europe. Keil's German *Introduction* was translated into Russian and became a basic handbook. Renan from France and Strauss from the Tübingen school were read extensively and replied to in the journals as well. The western Old Testament commentaries devoted to messianism and christological interpretations were also well liked.[50] On the technical and popular levels archaeology (e.g., the journal *Orthodox Palestinian Collection*, 1881-1914) and pilgrimages to Palestine were pursued so extensively that various tsarist governments built large churches and hostels at particular archaeological and religious sites to house their

---

48   Florovsky, *Ways*, Part II, Vol. VI, 122-24.

49   One might argue that Philaret envisioned an eventual evolution to liturgical Russian.

50   Florovsky, *Ways*, Part II, Vol. VI, 128.

traveling citizens. Further, no Russian sitting room was complete without a copy of the life of Jesus as portrayed by the world's masters. After the Revolution emigré scholars who survived the Bolsheviks and were able to make a cultural transition contributed anew to the societies that accepted them.[51]

VII. EPHESIANS 2:1-10

In dealing with this particular text there are notable differences between the way it is handled in the Eastern church and the way it is treated in the West. First, the pericope divisions used in the Orthodox church are frequently different from their Western counterparts, and this is a typical example. Ephesians 1:22-2:3 is the 219th epistolary pericope division, and Ephesians 2:4-10 is the 220th. Ephesians 1:22-2:3 is the prescribed reading on Monday of the sixteenth week after Pentecost and is read as part of the *lectio continua* for weekdays. It does not correspond to a particular gospel pericope. Ephesians 2:4-10 is part of the Sunday cycle of readings, read on the twenty-third Sunday after Pentecost. During this time of year the Sunday gospel lectionary is from Luke and does not correspond to a counted Sunday after Pentecost. Accordingly, Ephesians 2:4-10 does not always accompany the same gospel pericope from Luke.

What this means in popular terms is that Ephesians 2:4-10 is more familiar to the average parishioner because it is read on Sunday, whereas Ephesians 1:22-2:3 is read on Monday (and then only if there is a Divine Liturgy) and is most probably less familiar. In fairness to the reader unfamiliar with Orthodox liturgy, another item should be mentioned here. Although it is entirely in keeping with tradition for the homilist to preach solely on the lectionary reading from the epistle, in most instances—possibly ninety percent of the time—the preaching will be done from the gospel lesson, and the epistle might only be mentioned secondarily.

In addition, another presupposition about lectionary readings, East or West, should be "demythologized." In both traditions homilists,

---

[51] Aside from some of the names found in the bibliography one might include N.M. Zernov (Oxford), M. I. Rostovtsev (Yale), A. N. Grabar (France), and N. S. Arseniev (Germany and the U. S.), among others. Although none of them taught and wrote solely on the Bible, all of them made contributions in particular areas of its study.

ancient and modern, almost always treat the liturgical lectionary divisions—and sometimes the recent chapter and verse divisions!—as if they
are sacrosanct. They are not. From a "scientific" point of view, lectionary
divisions frequently do not follow the literary structure of the piece
being read, as one might expect. If one checks *any* lectionary today,
one will find numerous divergences from literary structure; and, by
the way, the divergences are usually intentionally included by the fashioners of that lectionary for a number of different reasons based on
liturgical need.

In light of this phenomenon the knowledgeable exegete is encouraged to be familiar with all the structures and substructures of the whole
literary work under consideration, and if possible, with the (hypoth-
esized) dynamics of the lectionary. In the case of Ephesians one has to
make some decisions as to how the repeated intercessions and doxologies fit together: the first begins at 1:15 and the second at 3:1, before the
main parenesis of chapter four. What might be inferred from the Orthodox lectionary is that chapters 1-3 are all introductory to the epistle:
a greeting, a thanksgiving, followed by two similar pairs of complex
intercessions and doxologies (1:15-2:22; 3:1-21), before the main body
of the epistle in 4:1-6:20.

Second, questions of translation arise: Which one is read liturgically?
Which is the best? etc. Not meant as a tautology, we may say that *every*
translation is only that—a translation. *Traduttore traditore*, "the trans-
lator is a traitor to his text," is a hard judgment, but partly justified.
Fortunately, all Orthodox seminaries in the United States still require
Greek (although not Hebrew and Aramaic, as did the old Russian acad-
emies). The preacher is expected to be able to speak with understanding
on matters of translation, vocabulary, word study, and so on. Laity
studying without ancient languages are encouraged to use and compare
as many modern English (and foreign language) editions as possible.
Liturgical reading in English is frequently done from the KJV, NAB,
or RSV, the last of which included scholarly participation from the
Orthodox in its preparation and received a hierarchical blessing. (The
NRSV is being given serious consideration as a study text, but is not
yet read liturgically.)

Third, one can expect the preacher's exegesis preparation, if not
the presentation of the sermon itself, to rely in part on the classical
homilies of the church fathers. For Ephesians, commentaries are available from several of the favorite Orthodox patristic homilists, including

St. John Chrysostom, St. Ephrem the Syrian, St. John of Damascus, and Theodoret of Cyrrhus. One aspect of classical patristic homilies, often ignored in recent decades, is that they addressed particular, sometimes recurrent, real-life situations in the Church. These sermons were generally not written in "ivory towers" or as exercises in method or style, though some of them were. The better ones were found edifying to the faithful at a certain point in history, an expectation that every homilist strives to fulfill in speaking to contemporaries.

Another aspect of patristic homilies that one learns very quickly is that there is no single "Orthodox interpretation" per se, but many good interpretations, all of which may be "Orthodox." It is clear when a church father lets the text speak on its own, and when he takes a position, doctrinal or otherwise, and uses the text as a "proof" of that position. (Significantly, patristic exegeses lack "faith vs. works" polemics.) In the latter case this is considered eisegesis (reading meanings into a text) rather than exegesis. Also, all of the holiest, most scholarly saints, are liable to make mistakes from time to time—a humbling, but also refreshing, fact.

Fourth, either of our two pericopes would normally be examined as to structure and form, as we observed in the translation guidelines of Philaret; but literary structure and form do not exhaust those categories, because the liturgical year also possesses various structures and forms which have an affect on exegesis. As a result, good sermon preparation is naturally sensitive to the liturgical season, the festal cycles (including hagiography), etc. Considerations of literary structure and form, nonetheless, have to be given a certain primacy. In our example, aside from the structural considerations mentioned above, one would also note that the epistolary form of Ephesians is different from that of a personal letter. Whether or not one insists on Pauline authorship, it is obvious that the form of a general essay or tract is more applicable here than one of personal direct address.

Fifth, it is common to give the passage a historical anchor, both chronologically and culturally. In the case of the Pauline corpus the historical parameters are rather closely set to one or another decade of the first century, whether or not one attributes Ephesians to Paul himself or to a "Pauline school" (i.e., deutero-Pauline authorship); and this knowledge about the first century is common enough that it does not bear repeating in sermon form very many times a year.

Orthodox New Testament scholars of the second half of the twentieth century have been conservative in giving up traditional Pauline authorship. (To their credit homilists, whatever their exegetical leanings, have not made Pauline chronology a focus of preaching.) We find this tendency to date the epistles early curious. The Orthodox should have no theological compulsion to establish strict apostolic authorship in order to validate the canonicity of a work—the question is hardly raised; and they have had little stake in the academic re-fighting of the Franco-Prussian War (the lines along which the early and late dating are usually drawn), which in any case seems to have subsided even among the French and Germans in recent decades.

Sixth, as we run the risk of oversimplifying for the sake of brevity, the competent Orthodox exegete employs one or another critical method to complete his sermon preparation. Whether the particulars of the methodological analysis would appear in the sermon presentation is doubtful. Although the historical-critical method is always important for an expert understanding of the pericope, methodological considerations may be restricted to sermon preparation only, because the method itself might not produce exegetical results that are edifying to the faithful—which is the classical raison d'être for preaching.

Seventh and last, and a part of the historical-critical method, is an analysis of what the pericope meant in its own historical and cultural context and what it means to Christians today. There is a tremendous amount of latitude in the application of each of these two analyses. In the case of the application of almost all critical method(s), most Orthodox Scripture scholars have taught their seminary students that the methods are, in themselves, neutral; and they should be used as tools, different tools working better for different tasks. Regarding what a passage means today, the prophetic demands of this principle might well dictate that the same sermon, given from a set lectionary, would never be given twice—every audience and time are deserving of a new response. Although this might appear overly demanding to American traditions in which the preacher weekly selects appropriate "proof texts" to be read in support of a prearranged sermon topic, preaching from the lectionary—and being open to the Holy Spirit—in the Orthodox church has not only discouraged personal theological agendas, but has exposed the faithful to the entirety of the New Testament tradition.

VIII. SUMMARY

In conclusion, the liturgical (including the homiletical) use of the Word of God in the Orthodox church may be seen occupying a preeminent place over the written word, used for personal devotion and study. In order to enjoy the "fullness" of Scripture and its referents, the average Orthodox Christian will look to the parish and monastic liturgical practice for the manifestation of this part of living Tradition. What a biblical text means today is primarily based upon church liturgical usage and proclamation in homilies, rather than upon ecclesiastical pronouncement. For the Bible to be "alive" in the Tradition, it must be heard and experienced liturgically—it is the Word which dwells in the heart of the people of God. When Scripture necessarily exists in a particular printed form or occupies hierarchical attention in edicts, these types of representations are only relative to the Word living among all the people, hierarchy and laity, now and throughout the ages. To say it differently, the living Word of God is seen manifest in the First Covenant, in Jesus Christ and his words, in those who repeated Jesus' words before they were written down, in the Church and her liturgical use of a written, "canonical" text, in the Fathers and Mothers of the Church, in contemporary congregations, etc.—ever showing forth a "present incarnation" of the living Word.

RECOMMENDED READINGS

Barrois, Georges. *The Face of Christ in the Old Testament.* Crestwood, NY: St. Vladimir's Seminary Press, 1974.

_____. *Scripture Readings in Orthodox Worship.* Crestwood, NY: St. Vladimir's Seminary Press, 1977.

Breck, John. *The Power of the Word in the Worshiping Church.* Crestwood, NY: St. Vladimir's Seminary Press, 1986.

Fedotov, George P. *The Russian Religious Mind.* Vol. I: *Kievan Christianity: The Tenth to the Thirteenth Century.* Vol. II: *The Middle Ages: The Thirteenth to the Fifteenth Centuries.* Edited by John Meyendorff. Cambridge, MA: Harvard University Press, 1966.

Florovsky, Georges. *Bible, Church, Tradition: An Eastern Orthodox View.* Vol. I of *The Collected Works of Georges Florovsky.* Belmont, MA: Nordland Publishing Company, 1972.

_____. *Ways of Russian Theology.* Part I, Vol. V and Part II, Vol. VI of *The Collected Works of Georges Florovsky.* Edited by Richard S. Haugh; translated by Robert L. Nichols. Belmont, MA: Nordland Publishing Company, 1979.

Jugie, Martin. *Histoire du Canon de l'Ancien Testament dans l'Eglise Grecque et l'Eglise Russe.* Vol. I of *Etudes de Theologie Orientale.* Paris: Gabriel Beauchesne & Cie, Editeurs, 1909.

Kesich, Veselin. *The Gospel Image of Christ.* Rev. ed. Crestwood, NY: St. Vladimir's Seminary Press, 1992. [The first edition included the subtitle *The Church and Modern Criticism.*]

Lossky, Vladimir. *The Vision of God.* Asheleigh Moorhouse, trans. Bedfordshire: The Faith Press, 1973.

Meyendorff, John. *The Orthodox Church: Its Past and Its Role in the World Today.* Translated by John Chapin. New York: Pantheon Books, 1962.

Obolensky, Dimitri. *The Byzantine Commonwealth: Eastern Europe 500-1453.* Crestwood, NY: St. Vladimir's Seminary Press, 1982.

Pelikan, Jaroslav. *The Emergence of the Catholic Tradition (100-600).* Vol. I of *The Christian Tradition.* Chicago: The University of Chicago Press, 1971.

_____. *The Spirit of Eastern Christendom (600-1700).* Vol. II of *The Christian Tradition.* Chicago: The University of Chicago Press, 1974.

Riasanovsky, Nicholas V. *A History of Russia.* 5th ed. New York: Oxford University Press, 1993.

Schmemann, Alexander. *Introduction to Liturgical Theology.* Crestwood, NY: St. Vladimir's Seminary Press, 1986.

Ware, Timothy. *The Orthodox Church.* Rev. ed. Harmondsworth, England: Penguin Books Ltd., 1993.

LUTHERAN INTERPRETATION OF SCRIPTURE
by
Joseph A. Burgess

What proof do you have? What evidence do you have? With such questions you are raising the problem of authority. And ultimately any discussion of the problem of authority leads to the question of final authority. What is your final authority? Archimedes said that if you would give him a place to stand on and a lever long enough, he could move the world. Christians will state that their final authority is God, Christ, the Holy Spirit, or the Bible. All Christians hold *sola scriptura* to be the final authority, even though *sola scriptura* may be modified by words such as "and Christ," "and tradition," "and experience," or "and reason."

Sola scriptura is the claim, yet what this claim means needs to be sorted out. One cartoon shows a package descending from the sky suspended from a parachute. The label on the package says "Holy Bible." Another cartoon has God sitting on a cloud and speaking through a megaphone; four tubes descend from the megaphone to earth, where Matthew, Mark, Luke, and John are sitting at desks writing down what they hear. We smile and dismiss such cartoons as caricatures. But at the opening lecture on the Bible at a Lutheran seminary the teacher picked up a Bible, placed it on the floor, and actually stood on the Bible for several moments. He intended to dramatize the fact that he took his stand on the Bible. The students were horrified for to them it was sacrilegious to use the Bible like this. After all, the Bible is a "holy" book, sometimes even venerated in worship. Somehow this paper and ink is different from all other paper and ink! Or is it? Has a concept of material holiness crept in from the Old Testament, where certain objects may not be touched or even looked at because they are holy (cf. Num 4:15, 19-20; 1 Chr 13:9-10)? Here authority has been understood as raw power. Only God, of course, has raw power in the ultimate sense, for he is omnipotent and no one can compete with his power.

At the other extreme *sola scriptura* means no more than that the Bible is an important document but one among many important docu-

ments. There is no word from the Lord, from outside of myself. Ultimately I have to depend on myself, my reason, my feelings, my
experience, or my conscience. At this point the uniqueness of the Bible
is lost because of "historical criticism." Historical criticism, to be sure,
must be defined. First of all, what is "historical"? Second, what is "criticism"? If historical means that there is no word from God, that the
only authority I have is my experience, then I am caught in relativism,
for reason, feelings, experience, and even conscience vary in my own
life and in the course of history. If criticism means that I am the judge
of all that is or is not, then I have made myself the final authority for all
things and once again have fallen into relativism. According to this, the
most virulent definition of historical criticism, the Bible has authority
only to the extent that I give it authority.

It is important to note that other definitions of historical criticism
are possible and even appropriate. What is needed at this point is that
you and I react to the assertion that there is no word from the Lord,
that the Bible is not unique, that I am the final authority. We know
that we are more uncomfortable with this assertion than the other extreme. Lutherans take the Bible very seriously, holding that it is the
"only rule and norm according to which all doctrines and teachers alike
must be appraised and judged" (*Formula of Concord*, Epitome, 1).
Lutherans differ, one must quickly interject, on how to apply this principle; some Lutherans even hold a view of the Bible which looks very
much like fundamentalism, although the vast majority do not belong
in this camp. But there can be no doubt about the centrality of *sola
scriptura* in the Lutheran tradition.

I. HOW IS THE BIBLE DIFFERENT?

Lutherans differ on how the Bible is different even while agreeing
that the Bible is the sole authority for all proclamation, teaching, and
life in the Church. No official Lutheran teaching on the inspiration of
the Bible exists, even though some have tried to derive a doctrine of
inspiration from the Lutheran Confessions. There is no official Lutheran
list of the books of the Bible, and for that reason the canon of Scripture
is in principle open for Lutherans; in fact Lutherans operate with the
same basic canon that most Protestants use, and it would be false to
imply that Lutherans have had any desire to add to the canon.

A. Is the Bible Different Because It is Inspired?

Lutherans take the Bible very seriously because it is the only source we have for God's word. But why only the Bible? What makes it different? Because the difference is not in the paper and ink and because the same words and sequences of words are used as in other literature, what possible claim can be made that the Bible is different? As is well known, the claim is that the Bible was written by the inspiration of the Holy Spirit and therefore the Bible is unlike all other books. Other religions also claim their holy books are inspired, but Christians claim the Bible is inspired by the Spirit of the one true God.

Every Christian holds that the Bible is inspired. The question is "how"? Various theories of inspiration exist, and each claims to describe the method the Holy Spirit used. No theory denies the Holy Spirit. For example, because Christians hold that everyone received the Holy Spirit through baptism, some would hold that the Holy Spirit continues to inspire the writings done by Christians. At the other extreme are those claiming that God gave the words, inspired someone to write, and that person simply held the pen.

There is no one biblical theory of inspiration; in fact, the Bible contains several theories of inspiration. Thousands of passages state "the Lord said," "thus says the Lord," "the Lord spoke," "the Lord spoke to," and the like. The difficulty is that what is meant is not obvious. Was the Lord speaking in such a way that everyone standing about heard? Or was the Lord speaking in such a way that the prophet alone heard, and in this case were sounds heard or were ideas registered? If ideas, were they filtered through the prophet's mind, or were they ideas the prophet could write down without being altered by the prophet's historical context? In all probability most of the writers of the Bible did not agonize over such questions but simply assumed that what they said and wrote was inspired by God. At times, to be sure, when it was a question of true or false prophecy and teaching, they did agonize and even provided certain kinds of answers (cf. Deut 13:1-5; 1 Kgs 22:28; Gal 1:6-9).

In the history of the first giving of the Ten Commandments on Mount Sinai the writer describes how Moses wrote down the words of the Lord, yet in the same chapter the Lord says he has done the writing (Exod 24:4, 12). In the history of the second giving of the Ten Commandments the Lord writes on the two tables of stone, yet Moses later in the chapter is the one who wrote on the two tables (Exod 34:1, 28).

How does one sort out the theory of inspiration in these passages? Only with great difficulty can a theory be proposed unless one resorts to complex explanations or unless editorial interference is suggested. In 2 Kings 3:15 the prophet asked for a minstrel to be brought; when the minstrel played, the prophet was inspired. This fits in with the mantic theory of inspiration in the ancient world. The musician was possessed and in this way inspired by the spirit. The prophet in turn could be inspired through the musician (cf. 1 Chr 25:1). In Zechariah 13:4-6 lacerations have been used by the false prophets to produce prophetic ecstasy, but the practice is found in official religious life as well (Jer 41:5; cf. 1 Kgs 18:28-29).

The most famous New Testament passage dealing with inspiration is 2 Timothy 3:16: "All scripture is inspired," according to the translation found in the King James Version. But the New English Bible translates: "Every inspired scripture has its use." This is at least a very acceptable version of the Greek text and brings out the fact that "scripture" in this context means the Old Testament. When one recalls the radical freedom with which New Testament writers make use of the Old Testament, one must be cautious about any theory of inspiration which would imply that the text was thought to be so holy that it must not be interpreted except in a very literal fashion. The adjective translated as "inspired" simply means "God-breathed," and no particular theory of inspiration is implied by the word. In 2 Peter 1:21 prophecy is not from human efforts, for prophets are those "moved by the Holy Spirit." Obviously this means that prophets are those guided by the Holy Spirit, but in what way and to what extent is not defined.

Paul distinguishes between God's words and his own words (1 Cor 7:6, 10, 12, 25, 40), but he does not describe how this is done or what makes God's words different. What does Paul mean when he writes "we impart this in words not taught by human wisdom but taught by the Spirit" (1 Cor 2:13)? Who is the "we" in this passage? Is it Paul, or is it an editorial "we," or is it all true Christians? Furthermore, what "words" are meant here? Are these Paul's words in this letter, or the words he uses in preaching, or is it the words used by true Christians when they testify? Similar questions arise with a phrase like "in the Spirit" (Matt 22:42; Rev 1:10) and the assertion that the Holy Spirit "will teach you all things and bring to your remembrance all that I have said to you" (John 14:26). How does the Holy Spirit do this, and to what extent? The conclusion from looking at the Bible on inspiration is that since no monolithic theory of inspiration is found in the Bible, the approach to the Bible should be doxological, that is, we can only approach the Bible with praise and thanksgiving because it bursts every category and theory we might have.

A brief survey of the theories of inspiration in church history shows how theories developed according to the historical context. Inspiration in the Old Testament usually meant that the personality of the writer was not overpowered by the Spirit but rather interacted with the Spirit. Christianity, however, came from the strand of Judaism called Hellenistic Judaism, which had appropriated the Hellenistic idea that the inspired writer has been used by God the way a musician uses a lyre or a flute. This mantic view of inspiration can be found in Philo, Josephus, 4 Ezra, and the Talmud. Christians used the analogy of the lyre or flute up to and including Irenaeus, but because of the rise of Montanism, which also claimed that its prophets had been mantically inspired, the mantic theory of inspiration came to be a sign of false prophecy. The mantic theory continued to be used as an apologetic device in battles against heresy, but during the Middle Ages for the most part a theory of inspiration was not emphasized because the tradition of the Church was the basis for authority.

The change at the time of the Reformation was not a new or renewed theory of inspiration. Luther took the Bible very seriously, as did others before him, yet he also could use the Bible very critically, as is well known, for example, from his statements about the Epistle of James as an "epistle of straw." The Lutheran *Book of Concord* did not prescribe any formal doctrine of inspiration for Lutherans. In the polemics of the second generation of the Reformation, however, mantic views of inspiration returned, for example, in Flacius Illyricus, who held that even the Hebrew vowels are inspired. During the so-called period of Orthodoxy in the seventeenth century, polemic fronts hardened and mantic views of inspiration became very important, notably in Gerhard, Calov, and Quenstedt among the Lutherans, and Voetius, "covenant" theology, and the *Formula Consensus Helvetica* of 1675 among the Reformed.

The synthesis which Orthodoxy tried to establish failed, for the modern world was breaking through. Not only had voyages of discovery found there are strong religions elsewhere in the world and Copernicus shown that human beings are not the physical center of the universe, but the Age of Reason culminating in Kant's philosophy raised questions about the place of religion in the total scheme of life. The French Revolution in 1789 challenged traditional political, social, and religious authority. In the nineteenth century Darwin produced a theory of evolution, questioning the uniqueness of human beings. Toward the end of that century Freud developed models of the human mind which challenged traditional views of human consciousness and drives. In this century Einstein's theory of relativity, Heisenberg's principle of indeterminacy, nuclear weapons, landing on the moon, and genetic engineering, to name but a few in a long list, have been further shocks to traditional authorities and beliefs.

Traditionalists, faced with what they perceived as relativism, scientism, historicism, secularism, and atheism, reached for traditional weapons. Roman Catholics worked out and then finally in 1870 defined papal primacy and infallibility. Anglicans produced the Oxford Movement. In the nineteenth century some Lutherans, such as Vilmar and Stahl, emphasized the Lutheran Confessions and a high view of the minister's authority. But the mantic theory of inspiration also was a major weapon Lutheran traditionalists made use of as they defended what they perceived as the true faith under attack by error. Other Lutherans adopted Reformed "covenant" theology ("salvation history"), according to which revelation takes place through the historical events themselves and therefore attacks made on the written text cannot affect the "inspired" events; already Bengel in the eighteenth century was famous for following this line of thought, and it continued in the nineteenth century in such theologians as von Hofmann, Rothe, and Mencken. A different tack was taken by Schleiermacher, who held that the Holy Spirit is identical with the spirit in the Church; for this reason the spirit which guided the apostles when they wrote is not essentially different from the spirit which guides each Christian today. The apostles, to be sure, would have a stronger measure of the spirit because they were closer to Christ's spirit.

Variations on these theories of inspiration continue today; no one theory dominates. All would contend in some way that the Bible is both human and divine, but whether this would be by analogy with Christ's humanity and divinity, an analogy already suggested by Chrysostom in the early church, would be a matter of dispute because not all would agree that since Christ's humanity is without sin, therefore the Bible must be without error. Does the fact that Jesus lived without sin mean that while walking he could not stub his toe on a rock?

B. Is the Bible Different Because It is Canon?

The problem of the Bible as canon is the unexamined ecumenical problem, a land mine waiting to explode. The general question of the relationship between the Bible and tradition, to be sure, has been discussed, as for example in 1963 at the world conference of Faith and Order of the World Council of Churches. But in spite of basic differences that exist among churches, ecumenical dialogues have simply assumed a consensus exists on the nature and extent of the canon. At stake is not only the fact that some hold the Apocrypha to be canonical and others do not. Rather, the nature of the Bible itself is decisive for all other theological questions. It can be said that Lutherans hold to the fact but not the extent of the canon because Lutherans are not tied to a specific list of books in the Bible. Yet what does it mean to hold to the fact of the canon? Within the Bible itself the word is used (Gal 6:16; cf. Rom 6:17), but how "canon" applies to the Bible is of course not spelled out.

The problems are complex. How do we deal with the fact that 1 Enoch 1:9 is quoted as prophecy in Jude 14-15? In 1 Corinthians 2:9, using the technical formula "it is written," which indicates authoritative scripture, Paul cites a passage not in the Old Testament. The letter of 1 Clement, written A.D. 95-96, the letters of Ignatius, written about A.D. 110, and the Didache, also written about A.D. 110, are not included in the New Testament canon, but 1 and 2 Timothy and Titus, written during the same period, are included. 1 Clement and the Didache were, after all, in some early lists and collections. What if the lost letter to the Laodiceans (Col 4:16) were found? Would we include it in the canon and if so, how would we decide? Would anything except an ecumenical council be able to make such a decision?

Lest we fall into the mistake of simply asserting that the canon is the canon is the canon and therefore the nature of the canon is self-evident, it is important to become aware of the various attempts in church history to define the canon.

1. **What is canonical is determined by orthodox content.** Where the spirit of Christ is, there is the canon. But where is the spirit? Where do we find orthodox content? The difficulty with this attempt is that it is precisely the canon which is supposed to define where the spirit is

and what is orthodox. Furthermore, in the early church, orthodoxy and heresy were not so easy to discern. In that early period lines were fluid. Only after long debate and struggle did orthodoxy emerge and heresy become evident. And in fact until well into the second century, all the baptized, having received the Holy Spirit in baptism, were understood to be inspired.

2. **What is canonical is apostolic.** But who are apostles according to the New Testament? Luke thinks of twelve apostles, the eleven plus Matthias (Acts 1:26), plus two, Paul and Barnabas (Acts 14:4, 14). In Romans 16:7 Paul writes of Andronicus and Junias who were apostles before him, in Philippians 2:25 Epaphroditus is called an apostle, and in 2 Corinthians 8:24 apostles are simply those who are missionaries. The New Testament books by Mark, Luke, and Jude are clearly not written by apostles, and if the claim is made that these men were closely associated with apostles, then already the understanding of apostolicity has been greatly widened. Very early questions were raised about the Pauline authorship of Hebrews; in spite of being associated with "John," the Book of Revelation was the last book accepted into the canon because its form and content did not match other Johannine literature and because it seemed to lend support to Montanism.

3. **What is canonical is early or the earliest.** To go back to the sources is not only an appeal to tradition, in this case the early or earliest tradition, but also an appeal to the humanistic principle that one must go back to the sources. What comes from the early church establishes the canon, or what belongs to the era of salvation history establishes the canon. Yet, as is well known, not all the writings from the early tradition have been included in the canon. Even if the earliest writings are more likely to be a more accurate reflection of what was said and done, some were not selected for the canon. The early church struggled with this problem, for some early writings, like Barnabas, were included and then rejected while others, like Revelation, were rejected and finally included.

4. **What is canonical is what the Church establishes as canonical.** If this were the case, the Church would be more authoritative than the Bible. Some would take this point of view. As a matter of fact, however, formal recognition of the canon by the Church took place rather late in the process. The first time that all twenty-seven books in the New Testament were listed was by Athanasius in his Easter letter in A.D. 367. The first formal recognition by the Church of this list of

books came from a local council—possibly at Rome in A.D. 382, certainly at Hippo in A.D. 393; another local council followed suit at Carthage in A.D. 397. Innocent I in A.D. 405 cited this same list. In some parts of the Orthodox church the Book of Revelation was not accepted until the tenth century. At the Council of Florence in A.D. 1442 the Roman Catholic church for the first time formally defined the extent of the biblical canon. As already noted, Lutherans have not formally defined the extent of the canon. The Bible of the Nestorian Church in Syria, the Peschitta, has only twenty-two books in the New Testament, while the Bible of the Ethiopian Coptic Church has thirty-one books in its New Testament canon.

Already in the second century the sayings of Jesus and letters of Paul had canonical authority, but it took centuries for the canon of the New Testament as we now know it to be established. Even the Gospel of John was not fully accepted until the end of the second century because it was suspected by some to have gnostic tendencies. If the claim is made that the Church establishes the canon, the question must be asked: Which church and at what point in history? Most important of all, however, is that those making this claim understand the Church to be more authoritative than the Bible.

5.   What is canonical is what has been used as canonical. The canon has simply developed; certain books have been used, and for this reason they have formed the canon. The difficulty with this attempt to explain the canon is that there has been a great deal of variety. At times Hermas, 2 Clement, or the Apocalypse of Peter was included. Why were the letters of Ignatius not used as canonical letters? To claim that usage makes a book canonical does not explain why certain books were used and others not used.

6.   What is canonical is what is found in the early creeds. For example, 1 Corinthians 8:6 and 15:3-5 are creeds or fragments of creeds used in the early church. According to this viewpoint such creeds are canonical; they are the final authorities for the Christian faith. Thus a certain pattern of preaching developed and became normative, a pattern of authenticity. Later, in the second century, Papias would claim unique authority for the sayings of Jesus. About this time the creed of the church of Rome also played a role in defining the Christian faith.

But from all the creeds and fragments of creeds, where does one find "the" creed, "the" pattern which is normative? In addition, one must ask if this attempt to establish the canon does not make the twenty-seven books of the New Testament subordinate to the creed.

7. **What is canonical is what the internal testimony of the Holy Spirit shows is canonical.** A woman told of the great spiritual blessing she received from the word "selah" in the Psalms. Yet scholars are not certain of the meaning of "selah"; it probably is some sort of direction to the conductor for the music. Does not this attempt to establish the nature of the canon ultimately mean my internal experience becomes the final authority? How is one to distinguish between the spirits (1 John 4:1-4)?

8. **What is canonical is the canon within the canon.** The canon within the canon is not the canon in a wooden sense. In other words, the canon within the canon is not a certain passage from the Bible, such as John 3:16, or a certain author, such as Paul or John or Matthew, or a certain book, such as Revelation. The canon within the canon is that which is used to deal with difficulties found within the Bible. The Bible contains such difficulties when it is taken literally. As a consequence, each tradition uses some kind of hermeneutics to sort out these difficulties. Each tradition has a theological approach to the Bible, an approach often described as the "hermeneutics of the gospel"; what is meant is that by this process the central truth of the Bible can be discerned and kept intact. In a sense the historical canon and theological canon stand in tension. The canon within the canon is not an authority by itself, separate from the gospel, the theological canon; and the canon within the canon is not an authority separate from the book called the Bible, the historical canon. Nevertheless, the hermeneutics of the gospel is that which determines the central truth called the gospel, and each Christian tradition has its own "hermeneutics of the gospel," its canon within the canon. A Lutheran "hermeneutics of the gospel" will be described in Section III of this chapter.

II. BASIC QUESTIONS AND PRESUPPOSITIONS

Christ is the answer. What is the question? The question might be: How does one decide that Christ is the answer? Or the question might be: What does it mean that Christ is the answer? Then all sorts of questions and presuppositions come into play. The point is that although all agree that Christ is the answer, not all agree on what this means. Nor does it help to claim to hold to Scriptures as absolutely inerrant and infallible in every detail or to claim to use a method of interpreting

Scripture that is literal and "historical-grammatical," instead of "historical-critical," for there is clearly no unanimity among those claiming to hold such positions.

But there is no unanimity among those claiming to use the historical-critical method either. Therefore some other criterion will have to be found for deciding whether the historical-critical method is acceptable for those holding to Christ as the answer. Those who attack the historical-critical method apply certain tests, and these tests are really the presuppositions of those opposing the historical-critical method.

A. The Presupposition of the Unity of Scripture.

The historical-critical method asks: "What happened?" What it discovers is not only that the Bible was written over many hundreds of years and in many different literary forms but also that the Bible contains a great variety of ideas, some of which at least appear to oppose each other. A famous example is the story of King David's census; in 2 Samuel 24:1 it is reported that the Lord incited David to take the census, whereas in 1 Chronicles 21:1 it says that Satan incited David to number Israel. Historical critics unravel the difficulty in these verses by noting that they were written by different authors at different times with different theologies.

Opponents of historical criticism presuppose the unity of Scripture. Is this a unity such as Christians posit for the Trinity, a unity which is finally a mystery? Or is this a unity which excludes contradictions, a unity built on logic, so that even if items stand in contradiction, a contradiction cannot exist because the presupposition of unity does not allow for contradiction? In that case the reader is expected to suspend judgment, to oppose his intellect, because of the supreme authority of the presupposition of unity. Most of the time, to be sure, the unity of Scripture is defended by means of an overarching concept such as the Word, or the covenant, or salvation history, or God's plan, or God's kingly rule, or God's grace.

The rejoinder by the historical critics is simple: How are difficulties solved by refusing to deal with them? More importantly, is it not in fact true that instead of working on the basis of the unity of Scripture, each stream of Christian tradition uses its own theological approach, its own canon within the canon, to sort out and solve the difficulties in Scripture?

B. The Presupposition that Reason is to be Subordinate to Scripture.

The basis for this presupposition is often 2 Corinthians 10:5: "We destroy arguments and every proud obstacle to the knowledge of God, and take every thought captive to obey Christ" (cf. 1 Cor 1:18-25). At first glance no one would fault this argument. Reason is not God, and reason cannot be superior to Scripture. Scripture tells us who we are and who God is, not reason. Reason can at best play a servant role, as a tool which helps us understand more fully what Scripture means.

The question, of course, is whether reason for historical critics is necessarily made superior to Scripture or whether historical critics do not also use reason as a tool. During the French Revolution, to be sure, reason was made into a goddess, and no doubt individuals have made reason superior to revelation. But for the vast majority historical criticism is a method, not a philosophy. In order to penetrate more deeply into the meaning of Scripture, it is necessary to think. Thinking always includes the use of the principle of analogy, for how else is it possible to comprehend at all? Surely no one would claim that Scripture must in principle be irrational or incomprehensible. Nor did Paul in 1 Corinthians 1:18-25 and 2 Corinthians 10:5 intend to reject thinking or trying to comprehend Scripture with the use of modern historical tools. Furthermore, modern thinkers are well aware of the fact that reason itself is part of history and subject to change.

C. The Presupposition that Miracles Happen.

But what is a miracle? The common understanding among those raising this question is that miracles are evidence or proof. By this they understand creation to be run by natural laws, like a clock; a miracle is that which breaks into such a world and in doing so provides proof that God has intervened. Some would also point out that the modern scientific view of the world as an open system allows for miracles, and others would also claim that through God's sustaining work everything is a miracle. As a result, the Christian faith can be defended as truth because there is evidence to back up the faith; few, to be sure, would deny that faith is also needed, but the important thing is that the proofs are there for all who are willing to see. And the proofs are there because the Bible records such miracles and intends them to be evidence and proof.

Those using the historical-critical method do not reject "miracles" in the sense defined above, for as defined above "miracles" stand outside of history and the historian can only state "I don't know." But the historian is able to ask the question whether the Bible intended "miracles" to be understood in the sense defined above. Not everyone who observed a miracle was convinced, and some said that Jesus did miracles by the power of Beelzebul (Mark 3:22). Thus it was well known that miracles were done by those who were not Christians. The Gospel of John has a very complex understanding of "signs" or "miracles" (cf. 2:23-25; 3:2; 6:26; 10:19-21; 11:45-48; 20:29-31). Paul indicates that demanding "signs" is one way the Jews show their unbelief, for Christians hold to the stumbling block of Christ crucified (1 Cor 1:22; cf. 2 Cor 12:9-13). The historian is also aware of the fact that literary forms sometimes give the reader a clue to the intent of a miracle story. The important point, however, is that the historian does not try to deny or destroy what the Bible describes; rather, the historical critic helps us understand the text and in fact helps us focus on Jesus Christ alone and him crucified (cf. 1 Cor 2:2).

D. The Presupposition of Facticity.

It is a fact that the modern mind often assumes that "facts" exist. What is meant is that a certain kind of information is demonstrable, directly accessible to the five senses, and available to all human beings. A popular view of science is that science is able to produce facts. Sometimes it is assumed that history also is able to produce facts and that the Bible, a book of history, is full of facts which Christians are to believe in. Historical criticism, in turn, is thought by some to be very destructive because it seems to question some of the facts in the Bible.

The trouble with "facts" is that truly modern science no longer claims to produce facts but rather statistical averages. And modern historical study no longer claims to produce facts but rather a record of interpretations and ideas. Even the person on the street knows that an accident at the crossroads will be interpreted differently by different witnesses. And even the person on the street knows that people in other times and cultures perceived and thought differently.

On the other hand, the person on the street still thinks that words have a specific meaning, a meaning which can be established by means of a dictionary after determining the context. What people do not realize is that dictionaries are history books, which is quickly perceived when someone looks into the Oxford English Dictionary, for example. Grammar is the same kind of problem. Most suppose that grammar is exact, that correct usage can be established. Some think that with a "historical-grammatical" method it is possible to avoid the perils of the historical-critical method. Yet grammar too is historical and depends on the philosophies of language operative at a specific time. In general it can be said that theologians need to bring the historical nature of words and "facts" to the attention of the person on the street.

E. The Presupposition of Propositional Truth.

Can truth be captured in a statement which then is "the truth"? After all, two plus two equals four. But I have never seen a "two" or a "four." Numbers belong to the unreal world of mathematics. In the real world we live in, life is historical and truth is historical. This does not mean that truth does not exist or is not truth. It does mean that even a proposition such as "God is one" must be understood as a historical proposition (cf. Jas 2:19). Who is God in this statement? What are the actions of this God? Furthermore, what is "one" in this context? Is it one over against the many? How does this fit in with Christian language about God being triune? What is at stake here is not a kind of new math, but what it means to be human, to be historical.

In times past theologians did hold that truth in religion could be stated in propositions and that the Bible contained propositions which Christians should hold to as the truth. That was because of the prevailing philosophy of the time, a philosophy built on a static, logical view of truth. But the Bible is not tied to any particular philosophy or any particular philosophical view of truth. For Christians truth is a person (cf. John 14:6) whom we know by faith. Truth is therefore dynamic, personal, relational, historical. Today the presupposition of propositional truth belongs largely to a bygone era. Even sentences that are propositions often communicate more by what they evoke than by what they denote logically. Thus the historical-critical method with its dynamic, historical view of truth and propositions is not a threat but a help in understanding what the Bible means for you and me.

III. A Lutheran Approach

Fortunately no one is saved by the correct interpretation of Scripture, or none of us would be saved. We are saved by Jesus Christ. Nevertheless, we need to discern who it is we believe in. How can we discern? What is the final authority? The Bible is the final authority, of course. The problem is that the Bible must be interpreted, for it must speak to all time as well as to its time. Who can authoritatively interpret the Bible? Is it satisfactory to say that the Bible is simply to be taken as it is because it is inerrant? But those who do this disagree widely among themselves. Is it satisfactory to say that the Church is to interpret the Bible? But there is no "church" to which all churches grant such authority. Nor can the matter be left to individuals, for they go their own ways. Lutherans propose a theological answer. Basic to Lutheran understanding is that the word of God is to be understood in three senses, in descending order to importance. First of all, the Word of God is Jesus Christ (cf. John 1:1-14). Second, the word of God is the preached word, the living voice of the gospel. Third, the word of God is the written word, the text of Scripture.

A. **Five Lutheran principles for interpreting Scripture:**
    1. **The New Testament interprets the Old.** In other words, the two testaments are not equal. Not only is the New Testament that which came later and therefore interprets the Old, but also the New Testament brings something new, Jesus Christ. Not only does the New Testament fulfill the Old, and therefore the Old Testament is to be taken very seriously, but the New Testament brings that which the Old Testament does not have, the cross and resurrection. The Old Testament, to be sure, describes the sufferings of Job, the suffering servant of Isaiah 53, and the laments of Jeremiah, but these are not to be compared with God's son dying on the cross in the New Testament. For this reason those whose faith is centered in the death and resurrection of Jesus Christ interpret the Old Testament through the New.
    2. **The clear interprets the unclear.** The converse is not true; the unclear does not interpret the clear. First of all, the interpreter is not to begin with difficult passages, such as 1 Samuel 2:6: "The Lord kills and brings to life," or 1 Corinthians 15:29: "What do people mean by being baptized on behalf of the dead?" Instead, the interpreter must begin with clear passages describing the human predicament and how God has acted; it is possible to place difficult passages in their proper context. But another step is involved beyond historical and intellectual clarity, for in the second place, clarity is that which points to Christ and whatever does not point to Christ is unclear; final authority is the clarity found in Christ. In other words, clarity is internal, theological,

and not historical or intellectual. At times Luther did, to be sure, argue for the external clarity of Scripture; that was in order to defend himself against "enthusiastic" opponents (Schwärmer). True clarity, however, is found only in Christ.

3.   **Scripture interprets itself.** But does this not mean that one is arguing in a circle? Does this mean that one cannot use other material to help understand Scripture? To the contrary! Every possible tool needs to be used in order to understand what Scripture has to say. Nor is Scripture understood therefore to be a perfect system, containing all knowledge and truth. What is meant is that Scripture is the final authority and cannot be subsumed under or judged by any other authority. Yet such finality is not finality in a wooden sense. Scripture is the final authority because it points to Christ, and nothing can be allowed to be a higher authority. Christ is the one who gives Scripture whatever authority it has.

4.   **"Was Christum treibet."** No satisfactory translation into English exists. Literally the words mean: "What drives Christ." What is meant is that what "promotes" Christ is the truth, that where one finds Christ, there is the truth. This may seem to be simply another slogan, like "Christ alone," yet it expresses in a profound sense the heart of the Lutheran approach to Scripture.

5.   **Interpreting Scripture can only be done within the Church.** This may sound intolerant. And it does not solve the question where "the" Church is. Again, what is meant is that Christ is found in and through his Church and that it is in his Church that his Spirit is working. A person might speculate about whether Christ and his Spirit are present outside of the Church, and if so, the definition of the Church would need to be broadened or what it means for Christ and his Spirit to be present might need to be redefined. All such speculation remains pure speculation. What the Christian knows for sure is that Christ and his Spirit are present within his Church and that those who are outside of Christ are, because they lack his Spirit, unable to interpret Christ correctly and therefore unable to interpret Scripture correctly.

It is obvious that all five Lutheran principles really state the same thing, that where one finds Christ, there one finds the truth and that this is how Scripture is to be interpreted. Finally this is a theological judgment. As a consequence, Lutherans not only have no problem with the historical-critical method but use it gladly when it helps point to

Christ and question the method and its results when it does not point to Christ.

The reader will object. Is it not impossible to believe in the "who," Jesus Christ, without also believing in the "what" about what he did and what he means for you and me? Is not therefore the historical-critical method to be rejected because it calls into question or may seem to call into question some or all of the "what"?

Lutherans take the "what" very seriously. As is well known, Lutherans take Scripture very seriously. They also take Christian tradition very seriously. Three ecumenical creeds, the Apostles' Creed, the Nicene Creed, and the Athanasian Creed, are all part of the beginning of the Lutheran confessional book, the *Book of Concord*. The *Book of Concord* is very specific about the "what" of the Christian faith and is, furthermore, full of references to the so-called church fathers of the Christian tradition. Finally, however, for Lutherans the question is "how" the "what" is used. Commitment to the "what" by itself could be a historical faith that has nothing to do with salvation. Christian faith is not only or primarily philosophical or historical truth. The important question is "how" such faith is part of a person's life.

B. **When Lutherans spell out this stance, they normally use five slogans.** Each of these slogans is like a miniature creedal statement.

1. **Christ alone.** Christ is the sole foundation, "the way, the truth, and the life" (John 14:6). Thus "the truth" is a historical person of a particular time and place, who did certain things and said certain things. Yet he is "the truth" who determines what all other truth is.

The difficulty is that although everyone agrees that Christ is "the truth," very different views of Christ remain. "Christ alone" remains a hollow formula. Nor is anything changed by holding that "the gospel" is the truth, for "the gospel," like "Christ alone," remains a hollow formula that has been filled with varying content. Therefore the alternatives are either to identify truth and gospel with the whole book called the Bible or to try to find some way to sort out the different views of Christ and gospel. No matter how much some claim to take the first alternative, everyone in fact operates on the basis of the second.

2. **Grace alone.** No one denies that salvation is by "grace alone." But what does this mean? Is grace truly "alone" or does it include works?

What about the law? Is grace to be categorized variously, as natural grace, actual grace, prevenient grace, and the like? Because of these difficulties, Lutherans make use of the Pauline phrase "justification of the ungodly" (Rom 4:5) so that grace truly remains grace and sin truly remains sin. Arguments remain, to be sure, about the "law" and "works" and "rewards," but the basic thrust of the Lutheran stance is made clear by the Pauline phrase "justification of the ungodly." Yet more must be said.

3. **Faith alone.** All may agree on "grace alone," but few agree on "faith alone." Is there nothing else except "faith alone"? Do no works apply? Yes, the Christian has no guarantees as the world reckons guarantees, for all experience, including the experience of faith itself, is ambiguous. Faith is based upon God's faithfulness to his promise in Jesus Christ, not on any security a person might find in the experience of faith or any other experience. Since through the promise a person is free from all demands of the law, a new world begins, a joyful life freely doing what others need.

4. **Cross alone.** Lutheran theology is cross-centered. The cross, symbol of torture and defeat, is the power of God for salvation (cf. 1 Cor 1:22-24). The cross without the resurrection is simply a tragedy. Conversely, the resurrection without the cross is simply a fantasy. Both cross and resurrection must be held as a unity. Yet as long as Christians continue in this world, their lives continue to be lives under the cross, broken by sin, sickness, weakness, and death.

5. **Scripture alone.** Would this be the place where Lutherans finally establish the "what" in some other way than by means of "theology"? Not at all. "Scripture alone" does not mean that Scripture in all its parts is equally valid. Precisely because Lutherans take Scripture seriously and in its literal sense, they take the difficulties in Scripture seriously, whether brought to their attention by the historical-critical method or by any other means. But Christ is the truth, not the difficulties.

Why should these five Lutheran slogans, all stating "Christ is the truth," be thought to be authoritative for the Christian faith? Could not other slogans such as "the church alone" or "inerrancy alone" be used just as well? And have not Lutherans with these five slogans tied themselves to "what" instead of "how" after all? But when Lutherans spell out their stance, they take one final step.

Final authority lies in the proclamation of the promise. To put it another way, when Lutherans are asked about the "what," their proper answer is to proclaim the promise that for Christ's sake all your sins are forgiven. The reason for doing this is that the question of authority is but the symptom of a deeper question, sin, and the answer is to proclaim the promise to you, not to present you with the "what" that supersedes all other "whats." And if you ask why this promise, the Lutheran will proclaim the promise to you once again. It is in the proper use of the promise that final authority lies; this is the "how." Final authority lies in the fact that through the Holy Spirit the promises are self-authenticating. As children Lutherans used to memorize Luther's explanation to the third article of the Apostles' Creed: "I believe that I cannot by my own reason or understanding believe in Jesus Christ my Lord or come to him, but the Holy Spirit has called me through the gospel...."

For all of these reasons Lutherans do not reject the historical-critical method. Moreover, a person cannot escape this method because it belongs to the very air we breathe in this century. It can help us better understand ourselves and Scripture. At the same time Lutherans are aware of the fact that the historical-critical method is itself historical and must be examined critically (just as each method is historical and must be examined critically). Finally whatever points to Christ is the truth, and what is needed is that the promise of salvation in Jesus Christ be proclaimed.

IV. EPHESIANS

Almost nothing hints at a concrete setting for the letter. Most satisfactory is the thesis that the original actually stated "in Ephesus" and that the copyists for some of the oldest and weightiest manuscripts, knowing that the contents of the letter do not match what the Book of Acts says about Paul and perhaps hoping to transform the letter into a letter for the whole Church, simply omitted the destination.

Did Paul write the letter to the Ephesians? The first and most telling reason for holding that Paul did not write Ephesians is the close relationship between Ephesians and Colossians. Larger patterns within the two letters are conspicuously similar. Most decisive is the use of similar terminology but in a different sense. Which letter was written first? Colossians has to have been first because it deals with a concrete situation. The author of Ephesians abstracted from that situation. It is difficult to imagine how the opposite sequence might have occurred.

The second reason for holding that Paul did not write Ephesians is theological. More specifically, the Church for Paul can be either the local congregation or the universal Church. He does, to be sure, think it important to agree with the mother church in Jerusalem and twice writes of the Church as a whole (1 Cor 15:9; Gal 1:13). Yet in Ephesians the Church always is the universal Church. According to Paul it is better not to marry because the end is near, although those who are married should stay as they are and those who lack self-control ought to marry (1 Cor 7). Ephesians paints an entirely different picture of marriage. It is to be a reflection of the perfect unity which exists between Christ and his bride, the Church (5:22-33).

The final reason for holding that Paul did not write Ephesians is stylistic. What stands out most of all is the lavish use of words; a freshman English teacher would say the style is redundant.

Taken individually none of the reasons against Pauline authorship may seem overpowering, but the cumulative weight of evidence becomes conclusive. Who then wrote the letter to the Ephesians? He was someone well acquainted with Paul's teaching and probably, because of his literary style and knowledge of Jewish tradition, a Jewish-Christian. More than that one cannot say. When was the letter written? Since Ephesians is dependent on Colossians and familiar with most of Paul's other letters, the earliest date is probably A.D. 80. Ignatius of Antioch, martyred shortly after A.D. 110, seems to be familiar with Ephesians (Eph 12:2; cf. Polycarp 5:1), which would set the upper limit.

Externally Ephesians has the form of a letter, with a proper opening, thanksgiving/blessing, intercession, body, and closing. In actual fact Ephesians is hardly a letter at all, for it is too general and theological. At the same time it is quite specific, aimed at mature Christians who are being asked to remember what their baptism means for the Church and their life in Christ. The best way to categorize Ephesians is to call it a liturgical discourse which has been put in the form of a letter.

V. EPHESIANS 2:1-10

At first glance this section might seem to be a break in the thanksgiving/intercession which began in 1:15 and continues in 3:1, 14. Yet the overriding theme of God's action in Christ continues, as can be seen by the way what is stated in 1:20 is applied to the Christian in 2:5-6. Redemption and forgiveness, mentioned in 1:7, is the theme of the first section of the second chapter, while reuniting all things (1:10; cf. 1:23) is the theme of the second section, and 2:19-22 picks up the theme of the Church in 1:23.

The structure of this section, and for that matter the whole chapter, is also based on the pattern "once—but now," found in succinct form in 5:8 but here spanning many verses. In modern America this pattern exists as well. We find it, for example, in the line "I once was lost but now am found" from the hymn "Amazing Grace." In New Testament times it is used in Romans 6:17-22, Galatians 4:8-9, Colossians 1:21-22, and 1 Peter 2:10, to cite but a few places. Its purpose is to bring out the contrast between past and present, between being without Christ and being in Christ, and as a consequence it is often connected with baptism. With thankfulness the Christian reflects on the evils of the past and the glorious certainty of his new status; at times an appropriate life in Christ is also mentioned. The words "once—but now" are not required for the pattern, for the contrast by itself is all that is needed. In verses 2 and 3 the word "once" appears as a clue to the contrast introduced by "but" in verse 4. In verse 5 the contrast lies in the content of the verse. Only in verse 13, after "at one time" (v. 11) and "at that time" (v. 12) have appeared again as clues, do the words "but now" actually appear along with another "once." In verse 19 the contrast again lies in the content of the verse. Nowhere else in the New Testament is this pattern used more frequently.

The Revised Standard Version of the Bible, a translation originally prepared under American Protestant auspices and widely used in Protestant (and some Catholic) churches, contains the following translation of Ephesians 2:1-10:

[1]And you he made alive, when you were dead through the trespasses and sins [2]in which you once walked, following the course of this world, following the prince of the power of the air, the spirit that is now at work in the sons of disobedience. [3]Among these we all once lived in the passions of our flesh, following the desires of body and mind, and so we were by nature children of wrath, like the rest of mankind. [4]But God, who is rich in mercy, out of the great love with which he loved us, [5]even when we were dead through our trespasses, made us alive together with Christ (by grace you have been saved), [6]and raised us up with him, and made us sit with him in the heavenly places in Christ

Jesus, [7]that in the coming ages he might show the immeasurable riches of his grace in kindness toward us in Christ Jesus. [8]For by grace you have been saved through faith; and this is not your own doing, it is the gift of God—[9]not because of works, lest any man should boast. [10]For we are his workmanship, created in Christ Jesus for good works, which God prepared beforehand, that we should walk in them.

The first seven verses are one long sentence, and the verb "made alive" does not occur until verse 5. "Walking" according to the flesh (vv. 2-3) is the first half of a parenthesis that is closed by the "walk" according to good works in verse 10. The first seven verses state the problem, which is sin, and the solution, which is God's action. The final three verses sum up what salvation by grace means, although a parenthetical slogan in verse 5 anticipates the summary.

V. 1. "And" is simply a connective. "Dead" refers, of course, to spiritual death, which is the most serious kind of death possible because it means being cut off from God. The cause of death is "trespasses and sins." No distinction should be drawn between these two terms, which both by the fact that two are used and that they are plural express the totality of sin. According to Paul's theology, sin brings about death (Rom 5:12, 21; 6:23; 1 Cor 15:56); he is referring, however, first of all to physical death. Nothing indicates that "you" is a reference to Gentile Christians. Rather, this is a description of the predicament which includes all, and "you" would normally be used in a letter at this point. The RSV has supplied the verb "he made alive" from verse 5.

V. 2. Three names, which are really the same name, are given for the evil force which opposes God. The first has been translated as "the course of this world" by the RSV. The phrase actually describes Aion, the god of this age, who according to the syncretistic thought of the Hellenistic world ruled all of space and time. "This world" stands in opposition to the "coming world" that God will rule. Another name for the evil one is "the prince of the power of the air." As in Colossians 1:13, "power" does not mean a quality but the sphere that the "prince" rules. The "air" is the lowest level of the heavens; human beings reach up into this level, for they either battle against evil (6:11-12) or are subject to it, as in this verse. The "spirit" is simply a general name for the same evil force. Each of the three names describes the totality of evil (cf. 1:21; 6:11, 16). This is the evil force that is "now" at work among the disobedient ones, leading them through sin to death (v. 1).

Thus by implication evil is not "now" at work among Christians and consequently they are free from its rule.

V. 3. A change is made to "we." Nothing indicates that Jewish Christians are meant, as some have claimed in order to support the thesis that in verse 1 "you" refers to Gentile Christians. "We all" is a shift to the inclusive style used in confession; we all confess that we are subject to sin, death, and evil. In addition, "we" anticipates the use of "we" and "us" in the following verses and may reflect Colossians 2:13. "Lived" more consciously describes life together (2 Cor 1:12; 1 Tim 3:15), while "walked" (v. 2) tends to be more individualistic (cf. 5:2, 8, 15). Only here in Ephesians does "flesh" have the negative sense it does in Paul. "Passions" and "desires" point to the abundance and complete-ness of sin, just as "body and mind," which could be translated as "flesh and evil thought," is the whole man in opposition to God. Radical sin in verse 3 produces an effective contrast to radical grace in verse 4. The concluding part of this verse has been one of the classical proof texts for the doctrine of original sin. Unfortunately the RSV has added "so," as if a conclusion were being drawn which could be considered a gen-eral principle, when in matter of fact this clause is parallel to the earlier part of the verse. What is meant is that since we too were dead in our trespasses and sins and enslaved to the prince of this world, we too were children of wrath like the sons of disobedience. "By nature" should therefore be translated as "really" or "totally" (cf. Gal 4:8; Wis 13:1). "Wrath" stands in contrast to mercy in verse 4 (cf. 5:6).

V. 4. "But now God has acted" is what the beginning of this verse intends, for the "once—but now" pattern applies here. The basis of God's action is his mercy, which is mentioned in 1 Peter 1:3 and Titus 3:5 in connection with baptism. Thus here also baptism probably should be understood. God's predestining love has already been set forth in 1:5 and Christ's very concrete love for the Church will be described later (cf. 5:2, 25). In verse 5 the words "were dead through the tres-passes" are repeated from verse 1 in order to bring out once again the contrast between our problem and God's solution. The shift back and forth between "we" and "you" in this verse and in verses 8-10 demon-strates that the author did not write at one point to Gentile Christians and at another to Jewish Christians. Such a hypothesis would become extremely complicated in this section! Instead the author made use of traditional slogans and materials which he did not follow slavishly, making it difficult for us today to determine exactly what is traditional and what is adaptation.

Vv. 5-6. That we were "made alive together with Christ" begins to apply 1:20 to us. Colossians 2:13 is clearly parallel to this passage. When were we made alive? The aorist tense points to a specific time in the past, which the parallel in Colossians 2:11-13 shows to be baptism. Paul would have written that we have been buried with Christ and that we shall be made alive and raised and made to sit at the right hand, but here nothing has been reserved for the future (cf. Rom 6:8; 8:11; 1 Cor 15:22, 52; Phil 3:9-11). This is very close to realized eschatology. It cannot be lightly dismissed as mere rhetoric occasioned by the enthusiastic joy that baptism evokes or as simply the description of Christ, the representative of the new humanity, already sitting in the heavenly places. The author fully intended to state that salvation is complete, even though, as in 1:14, he qualified his position and did not fall into the heresy condemned in 2 Timothy 2:18 or into Gnosticism.

In the middle of things the author adds a parenthesis that anticipates verse 8: "by grace you have been saved." The verb is in the perfect tense, indicating that salvation took place in the past and continues into the present. Paul did not use the verb "to save" in the past tense except for Romans 3:24, where the aorist indicating an event in the past is kept in balance by the future reference of the phrase "in this hope;" for him "to save" refers to those who are in the process of being saved yet will be saved at the last judgment (1 Cor 15:2; 2 Cor 6:2) and to future salvation (Rom 5:9-10; 13:11; 1 Thess 5:8-9). Understanding grace as the principle of salvation is very similar to what is stated in Romans 3:24, where Paul adapted earlier materials with a liturgical background, just as the author of Ephesians at this point adapted liturgical materials.

That we "sit with him in the heavenly places" is one of several very striking examples of how the author of Ephesians tends to think in terms of space instead of time. Even the pattern "once—but now" is really a description of two opposing spheres rather than progress across time. At times Paul did, to be sure, use space categories (for example, Rom 10:6; 1 Cor 15:47; Phil 3:20; 1 Thess 4:16), although he preferred time categories and occasionally a space category will also have a future reference (cf. 1 Thess 4:16). But in the letter to the Ephesians space categories have a decisive place, as in 1:3, 20-22; 3:19; 4:9-10, 15-16, and this passage.

V. 7. In spite of his preference the author of Ephesians, like Paul, used both categories. "In the coming ages" refers to the future. Tempting as it might be to understand the "ages" as personal evil forces in analogy to the "Aion of this world" in verse 2, elsewhere in this letter the plural has a purely temporal meaning (3:9, 11, 21). The plural form by this time had become customary through use in doxologies and simply meant "all times." Thus verse 7 means that in all future times God will effectively "show" (cf. 1:9) the "riches of his grace" (cf. 1:7) to us in Christ. Yet this verse must not be understood apart from 1:21 and the fact that Christ already rules the "coming ages."

Vv. 8-9. The parenthesis from verse 5 now develops into a short summary of Pauline theology. The summary is made up of Pauline slogans and as in verse 5 seems to echo the same sort of materials Paul used in Romans 3:24. The sovereignty of God's grace could hardly be confessed with greater clarity. But even though "grace alone" and "faith alone" are present, "saved" is once again, as in verse 5, in the perfect tense. Paul's eschatological dialectic of justification is absent where it is hard to imagine Paul himself would have omitted it. Two "not" phrases define what grace is: "not of ourselves," "not of works." Paul's polemic against the works of the law is nowhere implied. Where Paul spoke only of "works," his polemic was always implied (cf. Rom 4:2, 6; 9:32; 11:6). Ephesians 2:9, however, simply counterposes grace and every human work. Paul frequently warned against "boasting" (cf. Rom 4:2; 1 Cor 1:28-31; 4:7; Phil 3:3), which in its most insidious form is the claim to be better than others, so that grace is still not sovereign.

V. 10. In this context to be "created" is the same as what Paul meant by becoming God's "new creation" (2 Cor 5:17; Gal 6:15; cf. Eph 4:24). When did this new creation take place? Baptism could be meant (cf. Col 3:9-10; Eph 4:24), yet in addition before the foundation of the world God "destined us to be his sons" and to be "holy and blameless" (1:4-5, 11-12). In no way does this passage mean that Christians have been prepared to do good works, for it is the "good works" that have been prepared beforehand. But Christians will "walk" the way of good works because of freedom and gratitude, not because of an attempt to save themselves (cf. Rom 1:5; 6:16-18; Phil 2:12-13). That Christians "should" walk the way of good works is also intended by the author.

Conclusion.

Has anything important been lost in the translation of Paul's apocalyptic theology of justification by faith into ecclesiological universalism in the letter to the Ephesians? In Ephesians Christ clearly is central, as is grace. But Paul's eschatalogical tension between "already" and "not yet" has been greatly lessened. Already "we have redemption" (1:7), already "we sit with him in the heavenly places" (2:6). Therefore the need for ethics and battling the evil one (4:27; 5:6; 6:11-17) has been greatly diminished, in spite of the space these topics are given. The role of the law has become much smaller (2:15). For Paul the law is not exclusively a Jewish issue, but plays a decisive role in evaluating who one really is before God. The law, in fact, is a key to the polemic function of justification by faith. Ephesians is, of course, written in a different time and situation. The question is whether anything essential for Paul's theology has been lost when judgment and the law have lost much of their significance.

To put it another way: Something has changed in Ephesians. The Church has become determinative, and justification by faith takes second place. Is it important if the basic christological emphasis of justification by faith alone is lessened or even lost? Lutherans and those in the Reformation tradition have claimed that justification by faith alone is central and have been unwilling to allow ecclesiology to determine Christology.

IV. SUMMARY

Lutherans understand the word of God as Jesus Christ, the preached word of the gospel, and the written word of Scripture. The five Lutheran principles for interpreting Scripture are the following:

the New Testament interprets the Old;

the clear interprets the unclear;

Scripture interprets itself;

what "promotes" Christ is the truth;

interpreting Scripture can only be done within the Church.

The Lutheran stance is captured in the five "alones"—Christ, grace, faith, the cross, and Scripture.

RECOMMENDED READINGS

Barr, James. *The Bible in the Modern World*. New York/Evanston/San Francisco/London: Harper & Row, 1973. A challenge by a competent Old Testament scholar to all those who want to take the Bible seriously. The basic questions are raised.

Bornkamm, Heinrich. *Luther and the Old Testament*. Translated by E. and R. Gritsch. Philadelphia: Fortress Press, 1969. Technical and already an older book, this is an important contribution to the discussion of Luther's use of Scripture

Flesseman-van Leer, Ellen. *The Bible. Its Authority and Interpretation in the Ecumenical Movement*. Faith and Order Paper No. 99; Geneva: World Council of Churches, 1979. A collection of the documents and as such very helpful.

Krentz, Edgar. *The Historical-Critical Method*. Philadelphia: Fortress Press, 1975. The best short summary of what the historical-critical method is really about.

Kümmel, Werner Georg. *The New Testament: The History of the Investigation of Its Problems*. Translated by S. Gilmour and H. Kee. Nashville/New York: Abingdon Press, 1972. The classic history and summary of what has happened to the New Testament in the last centuries.

Neill, Stephen. *The Interpretation of the New Testament, 1861-1961*. London: Oxford University Press, 1964. Available in paperback and often reprinted, this book is a very readable introduction to our present day debate about interpreting the Bible.

Reumann, John, ed., in collaboration with Samuel H. Nafzger and Harold H. Ditmanson, *Studies in Lutheran Hermeneutics*. Philadelphia: Fortress Press, 1979. A modern debate among Lutherans about interpretation and Scripture.

Stuhlmacher, Peter. *Historical Criticism and Theological Interpretation of Scripture*. Translated by R. Harrisville. Philadelphia: Fortress Press, 1977. A recent attempt by a Lutheran to establish a more moderating discussion in historical criticism.

Theological Professors of the American Lutheran Church. *The Bible: Book of Faith*. Minneapolis: Augsburg Publishing House, 1964. A popular volume and still very useful for those who are facing historical criticism for the first time.

The Word of God: Scripture and Tradition. Lutherans and Catholics in Dialogue 9. Minneapolis: Augsburg Publishing House, 1994.

EVANGELICAL INTERPRETATION OF SCRIPTURE
The Background to Contemporary Evangelical Exposition
by
Grant R. Osborne

It is commonly believed among many nonevangelicals that funda-
mentalism-evangelicalism is a uniform tradition, characterized by a rigid,
atomistic, and static view of Scripture. Some have gone so far as to
caricature the movement as a "nineteenth-century heresy" which has
no roots in the Church before that time. For this reason it is important
to realize that wide diversity exists within the camp and to understand
the historical reasons why this should be so.

At the outset, I would assert that there are indeed historical roots
for the evangelical doctrine of inerrancy, which means that the Bible is
without error in its original autographs. Some among the evangelical
tradition follow the commonly held view that inerrancy developed out
of the application of Scottish Common Sense Realism to Scripture in
the latter part of the nineteenth century. This philosophy stemmed
from the inductive method propounded by Francis Bacon (1561-1626).
It entailed an optimistic epistemology which assumed that definite ap-
prehension of truth could be derived from an objective observation of
facts. Therefore, one could ascertain with certainty the exact meaning
of the Bible, which as divine revelation must be free from error. George
Marsden argues that the Old Princetonians of the late nineteenth century (Charles Hodge, Archibald A. Hodge, Benjamin B. Warfield) forged
their strong views on the basis of Common Sense Realism, "that the
Scriptures not only contain, but ARE THE WORD OF GOD, and hence
that all their elements and all their affirmations are absolutely error-
less."[52]

---

[52]   George B. Marsden, *Fundamentalism and American Culture: The Shap-
ing of Twentieth Century Evangelicalism, 1870-1925* (New York:
Oxford University Press, 1980) 113 (cf. 111-15), quote from A. A. Hodge
and B. B. Warfield, "Inspiration," *The Presbyterian Review II* (April 1881)
234. See also Ernest Sandeen, *The Roots of Fundamentalism* (Chicago:
University of Chicago Press, 1970) 103-31, and Jack Rogers and Donald
McKim, *The Authority and Interpretation of the Bible: An Historical
Approach* (New York: Harper and Row, 1979) 265-347.

However, John Woodbridge argues in response that Common Sense
Realism was a formative factor but not the source of the doctrine. He
states that while the Princetonians' view of inerrancy was reinforced
by Baconianism (see above), their doctrine of complete infallibility was
not "paradigm dependent" upon (i.e., it did not have its origin in) that
perspective.[53] Indeed Woodbridge's work is a lengthy compilation of
attitudes held by the Church throughout church history toward Scripture. He asserts, validly I believe, that while the exact formulation of
inerrancy or complete infallibility had not occurred earlier, the actual
details were to be found earlier. Rogers and McKim (see n. 1) and others had sought to demonstrate that the central position of the Church
had always been that infallibility was restricted only to religious or
salvific concerns and that it was not extended to particular details such
as historical or scientific statements. Woodbridge traces carefully the
viewpoint of the church fathers, the Reformers, and others, arguing
that they primarily followed a view of complete infallibility. On this
basis I would assert likewise that the fundamentalist/evangelical view
of Scripture follows the central position which the Church has held
since the first century. Note carefully that I am not here arguing that
this doctrine is correct, rather that it has historical precedent. The cor-
rectness of the position is yet to be discussed.

Modern fundamentalism/evangelicalism, however, does have its
primary roots in the late nineteenth and early twentieth centuries.
Throughout most of the nineteenth century, America was basically
conservative. In the post-Civil War era, in fact, it seemed that the conservative cause had indeed triumphed. Yet disquieting rumors continued
to surface, primarily the pessimistic conclusions of higher criticism from
Germany. These critical schools greatly influenced American scholarship. Ideas like Darwinian evolution and popular preachers like Henry
Ward Beecher were harbingers in the 1870s of a movement which would
soon cause a crisis and an intellectual revolution. It began in the universities and then spread to the pulpits. As conservative scholars retired
they would be replaced by younger, more liberal thinkers, often educated on the Continent. Moreover, American conservatives were
characterized more by practical piety than by apologetic concerns. The

---

53   John Woodbridge, *Biblical Authority: A Critique of the Rogers/McKim
      Proposal* (Grand Rapids: Zondervan Publishing House, 1982) 219
      (n. 88).

liberal preachers continued these pietistic emphases upon experience and morality as they sought to reconcile traditional views of Scripture with scientific views of reality. Preachers like Beecher and Lyman Abbott became exceedingly popular, and broader issues like the authority of Scripture were not truly understood.

The Evangelical Alliance, formed in 1846, became a major forum for debate. It centered upon revivalism, social concern (social justice, aid for the poor), Sabbatarianism (the sacred nature of Sunday as the "Lord's day"), free enterprise, and a high view of biblical infallibility. In 1873 James McCosh, president of Princeton, attempted to make Darwinism and Scripture compatible and occasioned a vigorous debate. For the next three decades the emphasis shifted to higher criticism. In 1908 the Alliance became the Federal Council of Churches, still primarily conservative but moving steadily to the left.

The evangelical response to the threat was quite diverse. Some retreated into piety and refused to get involved in such issues. Dwight L. Moody, for instance, refused to address controversial questions and simply preached personal repentance and the gospel. He believed that if one ignores error it will pass away. Here he alluded to Gamaliel's advice in Acts 5:38-39: "Therefore, in the present case I advise you: Leave these men alone! Let them go! For if their purpose or activity is of human origin, it will fail. But if it is from God, you will not be able to stop these men; you will only find yourselves fighting God." Many others, however (including direct associates of Moody's like Reuben Torrey), believed in direct confrontation. The term "fundamentalist" arose from a series of twelve volumes published between 1910 and 1915, *The Fundamentals*, though the title was first used by Curtis Lawes in 1920. These were written by conservative scholars to uphold the traditional views regarding the Bible and the cardinal tenets of the faith against the encroaching conclusions of "higher criticism" (e.g., denying the traditional authorship and dates of biblical books, questioning that Jesus actually uttered the "sayings" attributed to him in the gospels) and evolution. These volumes dispel the commonly held view that fundamentalism arose out of an anti-intellectual milieu. Indeed they attempted to "beat the higher critics at their own game," asserting that "higher criticism was not critical enough."[54]

---

[54] Timothy P. Weber, "The Two-Edged Sword: The Fundamentalist Use of the Bible," *The Bible in America: Essays in Cultural History*, Nathan O. Hatch and Mark A. Noll, eds. (New York: Oxford University Press, 1982) 109 (cf. 102-10).

One of the basic debates between fundamentalism and nonfunda-
mentalism concerned Bible study methods. The results of Common
Sense Realism on the growing conservative movement lay in the denial
of critical tools and the assertion that knowledge of biblical truth was
open to the average person utilizing only his Bible with the aid of the
Holy Spirit. Proof-texting, the practice of proving a doctrinal point by
alluding to a scriptural text, was deemed sufficient to establish a particular viewpoint. One of the most popular works in this regard was
Reuben Torrey's *What The Bible Teaches* (1898), which claimed to be
both "unbiased" and "scientific" as it documented (in five hundred pages)
theological statements with biblical proof-texts. The inductive method
of Bible study, proceeding synthetically from the whole to the parts
and seeking to elucidate major themes, came into prominence during
this period. The term "inductive study" in fundamentalism came to be
used for that method which studied the text by itself rather than critical tools or commentaries to elucidate its meaning. Yet it would be
shallow to hint that this was the only method. Conservatives like J.
Gresham Machen and Ned Stonehouse continued to interact with the
highest levels of scholarship throughout this era. However, the synthetic method did predominate.

Two further aspects should be noted. First, fundamentalism received impetus from a series of Bible conferences between 1876 and
1910. These centered upon both prophecy and apologetics, attempting
to demonstrate the "true faith" and to warn against the coming "apos-
tasy" (2 Thess 2:3) which was identified with the rising liberal movement.
The most important was the 1895 conference in Niagara, New York. It
adopted the five-point platform which later became the basis of *The
Fundamentals*: the inerrancy of the Bible, the virgin birth, the deity of
Christ, the substitutionary atonement (the view that Jesus died as the
sacrifice or "substitute" for man's sins), and the physical resurrection
of Christ and his second coming.

Second, the gradual control which nonconservatives established
over the nation's higher institutions of learning led to the Bible Institute movement. As their influence waned in the major seminaries,
fundamentalists developed their own schools in which the Bible was
the core of the program. Their purpose was to prepare church leaders
rather than to provide a broad-based education. Therefore, they es-
chewed the arts in favor of biblical and practical courses like pastoral
care or education (yet without educational theory derived from the

universities). However, this movement was not so much a retreat from society as it was an attempt to preserve the Bible-based education of the past. This came to a head in 1929, when J. Gresham Machen and Robert Dick Wilson resigned from Princeton and created a new school, Westminster Theological Seminary, in Philadelphia. From that time the separation was fairly complete, and for the next two decades there was little dialogue between the liberal and fundamentalist factions.[55]

One event which illustrates the growing rift was the so-called "monkey trial" in 1925 of John Scopes, a teacher of evolution in Dayton, Tennessee. The scene, trumpeted around the world by the press, pitted William Jennings Bryan, golden-tongued orator and four-time candidate for president of the United States, against the leading trial lawyer of his day, Clarence Darrow. The results are too well known to chronicle: Darrow not only demolished Bryan's arguments but also humiliated his views. From that time, fundamentalism was increasingly considered a backward, reactionary, and anti-intellectual bastion of rural Protestantism.

The ensuing years saw two developments within fundamentalism: a diminution of influence in broad sectors of American life and infighting among themselves. In the years of *The Fundamentals* there was a sense of unity among the Reformed, Wesleyan, and millenarian segments. In fact, we must correct the hyperbolic statements of Sandeen and others that fundamentalism was a millenarian or dispensational movement (the view that biblical history proceeded via periods or "dispensations" within which God attempted in various ways to bring mankind back into fellowship with himself). While this faction has become predominant among current fundamentalists, the origins of the movement were complex and included an amalgamation of many traditions. However with the increased controversies within each group, they lost contact with one another and in the 1930s began splitting into factions within themselves.[56] The concern for theological precision be-

---

55   See Louis Gasper, *The Fundamentalist Movement*, 1930-1956 (Grand Rapids: Baker Book House, 1981) 1-20 ("The Fundamentalist Heritage"), and Norman F. Furniss, *The Fundamentalist Controversy*, 1918-1931 (New Haven: Yale University Press, 1954) 117-88.

56   For reactions within the Arminian, Holiness, and Pentecostal sectors, see Vinson Tyson, "Theological Boundaries: The Arminian Tradition," *The Evangelicals*, David F. Wells and John D. Woodbridge, eds. (Grand Rapids: Baker, 1975) 38-57.

gan to extend to peripheral as well as cardinal tenets of the faith, and denominational splits multiplied, often over the issue of separation (from Christian groups not deemed sufficiently orthodox). Of course, there were more than doctrinal differences behind these wars. In a time of controversy, many strong-willed, charismatic individuals came to the forefront. The power plays among these leaders also caused many of the splits. It is fair to say that most of the vast number of small denominations today came into being in the late 1920s or the 1930s.

These internal conflicts as well as the poor image of fundamentalism caused it to lose public visibility and influence during the 1930s.[57] However, it would be erroneous to conclude that it was dying during those years. Statistics, in fact, show that it continued to grow, partly from the influx of immigrant groups who aligned themselves with fundamentalist concerns and partly from many Americans who grew disenchanted with the mainstream denominations. Nevertheless, discouragement was the order of the day within fundamentalism, primarily because they had no national voice but also because the splits had made the splinter groups small, ineffective units which could not perceive the growth within the scene as a whole. Moreover, the polemical, reactionary mindset which predominated was not attuned to optimism, that is, they centered upon the negative aspects of the movement and could not perceive the larger picture.[58]

---

[57]   George Marsden, "From Fundamentalism to Evangelicalism: A Historical Analysis," *The Evangelicals*, Wells and Woodbridge, eds., 147, calls the period from 1926 to the 1940s a stage of "withdrawal and regrouping," during which time sectarianism predominated and both separatism and millenarianism became tests of orthodoxy. This, however, was true only in the mainstream of fundamentalism. On the edges, for instance among many reformed Wesleyan and Anabaptist groups, this did not hold true.

[58]   See Joel Carpenter, "Fundamentalist Institutions and the Rise of Evangelical Protestantism, 1929-1942," *Church History* 49 (1980) 73-75. He argues that the four basic areas of fundamentalist activity (education, Bible conferences, radio broadcasting, and foreign missions) demonstrated "a growing, dynamic movement." There was no "American Religious Depression" in the 1930s but rather a shift of emphasis from polemics to evangelism.

In the 1940s a new group began to emerge, now known as "evangelicalism." It differed from militant fundamentalism along several lines: (1) a desire to dialogue with the world of scholarship, (2) a disavowal of radical separation (i.e., the view that one had to separate oneself from any group or person not espousing the "party line" in its details as well as in its essentials), (3) a greater theological openness on peripheral matters, for instance on eschatological issues, (4) cooperative evangelism, seen especially in the Billy Graham crusade in the 1950s, (5) a more eclectic education, as seen in the formation of Fuller Seminary in 1947, (6) a refusal to align flag-waving, political conservatism with orthodoxy, and (7) social concern, for instance the development of missionary agencies which primarily dealt with world relief and medical problems.

There are now two basic factions within the ultraconservative camp, namely the fundamentalist and the evangelical. The major issue which distinguishes the two is separation, which entails a more holistic set of attitudes regarding the Christian's relationship to the world and other Christian groups. In many cases the use of the Bible is very similar, especially on the popular level. Both groups tend to proof-text and to atomize Scripture (see further below). Yet with respect to external aspects they differ markedly. The fundamentalists tend to take a negative approach to other Christian groups and to such "worldly" amusements as movies, cards, dancing, etc. Moreover, they are often characterized by "second-degree separation," i.e., severance not only from the world of liberalism but also from evangelicals who refuse to detach themselves from such. The classic example is the fundamentalist opposition to Billy Graham because of his openness to "liberal" participation in his crusades. The evangelical, on the other hand, is more open to such things as movies or recreation on Sunday. Furthermore, there is a desire to dialogue with other Christian movements and to cooperate where such does not compromise the basic tenets of evangelical dogma (see the seven points above). Evangelicals participate in the Society of Biblical Literature and attend meetings of the National Council of Churches (although there is great debate regarding the extent of participation in the latter).

The break between the two can be seen, for instance, in the rival national organizations. In September 1941, Carl McIntire formed the American Council of Christian Churches (ACCC) and in October of that year another conference was held at Moody Bible Institute to form the National Association of Evangelicals. The former organization specifically wished to combat the Federal Council of Churches while the latter did not demand that their members sever all ties. While the two groups had quite similar views with respect to Scripture and other doctrines, they differed greatly in terms of attitudes toward outsiders (see the previous paragraph).

However, other splinter movements within the two groups have occurred. Fundamentalism has seen several splits, for example that between McIntire and Bob Jones. Jerry Falwell has been moving more toward the evangelical camp in his rhetoric, although many of his political statements are geared to the fundamentalist.[59] The ACCC split a few years ago between a moderate faction and a McIntire-led splinter group. The current organization is controlled by the moderates.

Evangelicalism is also divided primarily on the issue of inerrancy. The debate has been chronicled in the two works of Harold Lindsell,[60] which unfortunately are highly polemical. The Evangelical Theological Society, organized in 1949 to provide an eclectic forum for theological discussion, has made inerrancy its only doctrinal statement so as to provide a platform for differences on other matters. In recent years, however, it has been divided on a definition and criteria for inerrancy. As a result, another organization, the International Council on Biblical Inerrancy (ICBI) has been formed to adjudicate a more carefully defined statement on the issue. Those who affirm the doctrine of total infallibility/inerrancy are now subdivided into two further groups, one segment seeking to establish criteria for deciding what affirms the doctrine and another wishing to allow flexibility in determining details.

This, of course, is not to intimate that inerrancy is the sole or even the major dividing factor among evangelicals. Many other factors (e.g., high versus low forms of worship, eschatological views, the charismatic issue, the sacraments, women in the Church, ethical issues, Calvinism versus Arminianism versus Anabaptism) could be mentioned. However, inerrancy most clearly relates to the use of Scripture and currently is a major contention. The 1982 meeting of the Evangelical Theological

[59]   See Jerry Falwell, *The Fundamentalist Phenomenon: The Resurgence of Conservative Christianity* (Garden City, NY: Doubleday, 1981).

[60]   Harold Lindsell, *Battle for the Bible* (Grand Rapids: Zondervan, 1976), and *The Bible in theBalance* (Grand Rapids: Zondervan, 1979).

Society (December 15-17, 1982) centered upon "biblical criticism" and concluded with a basic affirmation of critical tools when used moderately, i.e, as a means of interpreting a passage rather than determining the degree of authenticity.

I. THE EVANGELICAL AND SCRIPTURE

As one might determine from the preceding discussion, there is wide diversity among evangelicals with respect to their use of Scripture. Many segments of the various camps do indeed employ an atomistic, proof-texting approach and strongly disparage the use of tools like commentaries or background literature, saying that they invariably focus upon problems of interpretation and inevitably move one away from a commitment to the "simple gospel." This relic of "common sense realism" is still prevalent. However, the interest in a proper approach to the Bible is certainly growing, as witness the recent upsurge in evangelical works on Bible study methods or hermeneutics. To be certain, many books go no further than inductive Bible study. However, others are extremely sophisticated and aware of the enormous body of literature, secular and religious, on the problem of literary interpretation. J. Robertson McQuilkin, president of Columbia Bible College, says, "Even an introductory textbook on hermeneutics ought to be...thoroughly grounded in solid scholarship...."[61] It is very clear that McQuilkin and others deny the validity of proof-texting. Walter Kaiser states that "'prooftexting,' the isolation and use of verses apart from their immediate or sectional content, is reprehensible and should be discontinued immediately."[62] Recent graduates of evangelical schools have had strong courses in proper exegetical procedure.

---

[61] J. Robertson McQuilkin, *Understanding and Applying the Bible* (Chicago: Moody Press, 1983) 10. See also J. I. Packer, "Infallible Scripture and the Role of Hermeneutics," *Scripture and Truth*, D. A. Carson and John D. Woodbridge, eds. (Grand Rapids: Zondervan, 1983) 325-56, who speaks of "the centrality of hermeneutics to day (325-27).

[62] Walter Kaiser, *Toward an Exegetical Theology* (Grand Rapids: Baker, 1981) 82. He clarifies this by arguing that a misuse of the "analogy of faith," in which a future passage is utilized to interpret a previous one, is equally wrong.

A. Meaning and the Author-Text-Reader Problem.

Evangelicals traditionally stress "what it meant" as well as "what it means." There is strong unanimity with respect to intentionality, i.e., the possibility of recovering the author's intended meaning. The modern hermeneutical dilemma stems from the relation between author, text, and reader. The author creates the text in order to communicate a certain intended message. The reader searches the text in order to discover a message, and it is here that the problem occurs. The author is not present to clarify the intended meaning, and readers often find quite different meanings in the text. Inherent in this is the difficulty of preunderstanding, of moving behind one's own preconceived notions to enter into the thought-world of the text. When one goes the next step and seeks to discover the author's intended meaning, the task becomes immeasurably more complex. As a result, many literary schools posit the autonomy of the text from the author and to a greater or lesser degree pronounce the impossibility of ascertaining the "author's intended meaning." Instead, the focus has shifted to the reader, and theories of "polyvalence" or "multiple meanings" predominate. As one enters the world of the text, a hermeneutical circle occurs in which both text and reader are altered. While total subjectivity does not result, the dynamic transference of meaning allows many possible interpretations to occur depending on the context or perspective of the reader.[63]

While recognizing the thorny problems involved in the task of interpretation, evangelicals are not so pessimistic regarding the task of determining the intended meaning. While there is no space to present detailed arguments, I might mention a few salient points. At the outset, the work of the literary critic E. D. Hirsch has become very popular. Building upon Wittgenstein's theory of "family resemblances" between "language games," Hirsch argues that understanding is connected to "intrinsic genre," that is, the "type of utterance" which narrows down the "rules" that apply to a particular speech. While preunderstanding plays a major role in interpretation, there is a basic genre which is

---

[63] For good discussions of this, see Charles M. Wood, *The Formation of Christian Understanding. An Essay in Theological Hermeneutics* (Philadelphia: Westminster, 1981), and David H. Kelsey, *The Uses of Scripture in Recent Theology* (Philadelphia: Fortress Press, 1975). Kelsey has a "functional" view of authority which sees Scripture as providing "patterns" rather than concepts.

intrinsic to a literary work and which, when discovered, can lead to a correct delineation of its original intended meaning.[64]

Hirsch separates meaning (what it meant) and significance (what it means) into two separate aspects of the hermeneutical task. The issue is whether one can get behind the latter to the former. After lengthy discussion of the problem of semantics and meaning, Moises Silva is convinced that one can: "I take it as a valid assumption that the interpreter approaches any text with a multitude of experiences...that inform his or her understanding of that text....But I believe just as strongly that the interpreter may *transcend*, though not eliminate, that point of reference.... The moment we look at a text we contextualize it, but a self-awareness of that fact opens up the possibility of modifying our point of reference in the light of contradictory data."[65]

A connected issue relates to the questions of biblical authority and propositional revelation in Scripture, i.e., that the Bible is the actual Word of God in propositional form rather than a witness to God's revelation. Paul Achtemeier asserts that a concern for an infallible, propositional revelation has led to the type of harmonizing (in order to solve discrepancies) which in effect is self-contradictory, since it creates more problems than it solves.[66] He therefore proposes a dynamic model which views inspiration as a process involving not only the original tradition but later situations and respondents. Interestingly, the type of "glib harmonization" which Achtemeier attacks is also denied by

[64]   E. D. Hirsch, *Validity in Interpretation* (New Haven: Yale University Press, 1967) 72-88. For a slightly different proposal, centering on the text rather than the author, see P. D. Juhl, *Interpretation: An Essay in the Philosophy of Literary Criticism* (Princeton: Princeton University Press, 1980) 12-15. Two who follow closely this argument are Walter Kaiser, "The Single Intent of Scripture," *Evangelical Roots* Kenneth Kantzer, ed. (Nashville: Thomas Nelson, 1978), and Elliott Johnson, *Hermeneutics* (Grand Rapids: Zondervan, forthcoming).

[65]   Moises Silva, *Biblical Words and Their Meaning: An Introduction to Lexical Semantics* (Grand Rapids: Zondervan, 1983) 148. See also William W. Klein, Craig L. Blomberg, Robert L. Hubbard, Jr., *Introduction to Biblical Interpretation* (Dallas: Word Books, 1993) 132-34.

[66]   Paul Achtemeier, *The Inspiration of Scripture: Problems and Proposals* (Philadelphia: Westminster, 1980) 57-75.

D. A. Carson, who nevertheless argues further that the method when utilized as one among many literary tools can be highly useful.[67]

To return to the subject of propositional revelation, Wayne Grudem provides an extensive discussion of Scripture's "self-attestation," arguing (1) that all of the Old Testament writings are considered God's words, (2) that the written words of God have the same truth-status as the spoken words of God, and (3) that the New Testament writings attained the same status as the Old Testament writings.[68] He concludes this after examining introductory formulas and claims to authority within the biblical text. The implications are crucial for the evangelical claim to propositional revelation. If Grudem's findings are correct, the Bible claims to *be* the Word of God, not only to testify to the Word of God. Moreover, the Bible would demand to be understood in terms of its original meaning, not merely be open to multiple meanings in various contexts. This is at the heart of the evangelical view of Scripture. I also concur with Anthony C. Thiselton's excellent discussion of authority and the Bible's "language games." He argues that both static and dynamic views are valid: The Bible is more than "a handbook of information and description" in that it embraces a "whole range of dynamic speech-acts"; yet at the same time this performative element rests "on the truth of certain states of affairs in God's relation to the world."[69] Few evangelicals would argue for a purely static view of Scripture. Most would see both static and dynamic elements, which we might align with meaning and significance.

In recent evangelical hermeneutics, the importance of the reader as interpreter is increasingly recognized. Klein, Blomberg, and Hubbard

---

[67]   D. A. Carson, "Unity and Diversity in the New Testament: The Possibility of Systematic Theology," *Scripture and Truth*, Carson and Woodbridge, eds, 90-93 (cf. 139-41).

[68]   Wayne A. Grudem, "Scripture's Self-Attestation and the Problem of Formulating a Doctrine of Scripture," *Scripture and Truth*, 49 (cf. 19-59).

[69]   A. C. Thiselton, *The Two Horizons: New Testament Hermeneutics and Philosophical Description* (Grand Rapids: Eerdmans, 1980) 437 (cf. 432-38). See also his *New Horizons in Hermeneutics: The Theory and Practice of Transforming Biblical Reading* (Grand Rapids: Zondervan, 1992) 597-619.

see three aspects in literary criticism: "(1) focus on the author's intent in composing the text, (2) the conventions of the text that reflect that intent, and (3) the reader's response to the text."[70] All these elements interact in the production of meaning. Yet how does the reader align with the intended meaning of the text? Thiselton believes that the text performs a transforming function, guiding the readers to the new horizons or life-worlds of the text and controlling the participation of the reader in the text.[71] I see author, text, and reader engaging in a trialogue in coming-to-understanding. While the author produces the text, it is the text not the author that the reader studies. Readers participate in authorial/textual meaning by studying the exegetical aspects (context, grammar, semantics, background) that provide clues to meaning and then by listening to and participating in the demands of the text. As readers we recognize the guiding influence of our preunderstanding but place this in front of the text (with the text guiding the production of meaning) rather than behind the text (with us controlling the text).[72]

B. Literary Criticism.

The first stage of evangelical criticism obviously deals with the larger questions of genre, plot, narrative structure, and thought development. The best control over the tendency to atomize individual statements is constant cognizance of the entire context within which assertions are found. Thus serious Bible study begins with rhetorical criticism, the study of the logical patterns which characterize the total message. Some textbooks on hermeneutical theory have discussed genre under the rubric "special revelation." However, these texts are seldom holistic on genre, for while traditional aspects like figures of speech, parables, and apocalyptic are discussed, there is seldom coverage of gospels or narrative hermeneutics. An excellent work which rectifies this is *How to Read the Bible for All Its Worth* by Gordon D. Fee and Douglas Stuart, with successive chapters on the basic genres: the epistles,

---

[70]   Klein, Blomberg, Hubbard, *Biblical Interpretation*, 136.

[71]   Thiselton, *New Horizons*, 611-19.

[72]   See my *The Hermeneutical Spiral: A Comprehensive Introduction to Biblical Interpretation* (Downers Grove, IL: InterVarsity Press, 1991) 310-11.

Old Testament narratives, Acts, the Gospels, parables, the law(s), the prophets, the Psalms, wisdom, and Revelation.

Genre has come increasingly to the fore in recent debates on the gospels. Not only has a plethora of works appeared on the gospel genre, but also it has led to several studies purporting to interpret the gospel narratives on the basis of generic considerations. This may best be exemplified by Robert Gundry's commentary on Matthew.[73] He states that some of the Matthean portions of this gospel (e.g., the magi) are not historical but are "creative midrash," Jewish fictional pieces which were meant to be interpreted as such by his Jewish audience. However, many feel that Gundry has not defined midrash properly nor has he applied proper parallels. Genre must first be identified correctly and then the characteristics must be drawn adequately between the pieces of literature.

Once the genre has been isolated, an ever-narrowing series of concentric approaches delve deeper and deeper into the text. Here the evangelical hermeneutic demonstrates an affinity with modern trends, as recent schools (e.g., structuralism, canon criticism, rhetorical criticism) have moved away from a stress on the parts (the error of form criticism) to the centrality of the whole. Literary criticism assumes that the "world of the text" as well as historical-critical concerns is a valid source for study. The symmetry of the final product therefore is a primary focus, and evangelical approaches have historically stressed this contextual aspect. Interestingly, the major Bible study approach stemming from the "Common Sense Realism" school at the turn of the century was the synthetic method described in James Gray's *How to Master the Bible* (1904), which assumed the priority of the whole.[74]

This remains the core of modern-day inductive methodology, which begins by charting the whole structure of a book, delineating the pat-

---

[73]   Robert Gundry, *Matthew: A Commentary on His Literary and Theological Art* (Grand Rapids: Eerdmans, 1981). See my review article in *TSF (Theological Students Fellowship) Bulletin* 6/4 (March-April 1983) 1416, which relates the comments of the symposia on his work at ETS and AAR in December 1982.

[74]   See the discussion in Weber, "The Two-Edged Sword," *The Bible in America*, 111-14. Weber describes this synthetic method in this way: "Once the whole was in hand, one could turn one's attention to a more detailed study of its component parts..." (112-13).

tern of its argumentation and its major themes. Without the sophisticated study of compositional techniques exhibited in the world of academia, the inductivist still seeks the interplay of narrative factors in the text. Evangelical scholars are more and more being trained in literary theory and producing works in this field. Yet the so-called "fictive" (rhetorical schools argue that all narratives have the basic elements of "fiction," i.e., plot, structure, character, conflict) components stemming from the school of narrative hermeneutics are strongly criticized for the facile assumptions regarding the aesthetic element of Scripture. Evangelicals would want to restrict fictive factors to that genre rather than extend them to historical and didactic portions of the Bible. With respect to parables, for instance, evangelicals would utilize modern parable research regarding the complexity of the interpretive task but would still seek the intended meaning of the parable in its setting as opposed to the multiple meanings attributed by structuralists. However, they would differ in other respects, with some still holding to the "single meaning" approach of Jülicher and Jeremias,[75] but with others taking a modified "allegorical" approach.[76]

C. Textual Criticism.

Evangelicals, with their stress on the propositional content of Scripture, are naturally very concerned to ascertain the original words of the biblical text. The description of the task by Professor Harrington is very similar to that employed by evangelicals.[77] Issues, however, are slightly different. One major debate between fundamentalists and evangelicals centers upon the *textus receptus*, the "received text" developed by Erasmus and that behind the King James Bible. Those behind the "King James only" movement argue for the "majority text," i.e., the text supported by the majority of the ancient manuscripts. However, since most exemplars copied before A.D. 800 have been destroyed,

[75] See Robert H. Stein, *An Introduction to the Parables of Jesus* (Philadelphia: Westminster, 1981).

[76] See my *Hermeneutical Spiral*, 235-49, and Craig Blomberg, *Interpreting the Parables* (DownersGrove, IL: InterVarsity Press, 1990). This holds that Jesus utilized allegory in his parables, and that there is no "single" thrust, but several theological thrusts in Jesus' parables.

[77] See the chapter by Daniel Harrington in this volume.

the majority of evangelical scholars accept the eclectic method developed by Westcott and Hort rather than the "received text."

In spite of the commitment to the text, however, there is also a paucity of evangelical text-critics. Many have done text-critical research in their doctoral work, largely due to the fact that several graduate programs will not allow exegetical studies from an evangelical perspective. However, few follow up this program with further text-critical research. The reasons given by Professor Harrington for the poor state of textual criticism in Catholic circles apply also to the evangelical situation.

D. The Historical-Critical Method.

There is a great debate in both evangelical and nonevangelical circles regarding the validity of historical-critical research. The pessimism of the approach and the absence of constructive results have made scholars from many traditions leery about its value. However, one must differentiate various aspects of a particular method and avoid labeling the entire school by its negative characteristics. This is the debate within evangelicalism at the present time. Both form and redaction criticism have been closely identified with tradition criticism, which tends to determine the authenticity of a pericope or story on the basis of its form. If the saying or story is simple rather than complex, it is more likely to be authentic, that is, to stem from the historical Jesus rather than the later church. These scholars theorize that the needs of the Church were read back onto the lips of Jesus. Tradition critics tend to determine the authenticity of Jesus' sayings in the gospels on the basis of three criteria:[78] (1) dissimilarity, which assumes that a saying is authentic only if it cannot be paralleled either in Judaism or in the early church, (2) multiple attestation, which views a saying/pericope as authentic if it can be traced through several sources or layers of tradition, and (3) coherence, which accepts a tradition that is consistent with passages which have already been authenticated. However, the philosophical skepticism behind these has been challenged from many quarters, and the approach is unacceptable to evangelicals.

---

[78]   For evangelical responses, see my "The Evangelical and *Traditionsgeschichte*" in *The Journal of the Evangelical Theological Society* 21/2 (1978) 117-30, and R. H. Stein, "The 'Criteria' for Authenticity," *Gospel Perspectives I*, R. T. France and David Wenham, eds. (Sheffield: JSOT Press, 1980) 225-63.

Some believe that such methodological problems belie the method as whole.[79] They argue for a historical-theological rather than a historical-critical method on the grounds that the former is in closer proximity to the biblical view of itself. The reconstruction of the "original event" is viewed as a speculative enterprise which can never provide a constructive alternative to the text as it is. Others, like the canon critics, accept the criticisms but assert that one must not take a "naive" approach to the text. Evangelicalism is divided on the issue, although I admit that I stand more closely to the latter position.

Redaction criticism is a case in point. While form criticism sought the *Sitz im Leben* or social matrix from which various strata of tradition stemmed, redaction criticism has studied the final author's contribution. In so doing, many critics have assumed that only those segments peculiar to an individual evangelist carry his imprimatur. However, such a supposition lacks proof, for the biblical writers used the traditions themselves as well as additions/omissions in presenting their messages. Moreover, most evangelicals are not so settled on the classical form of the documentary hypothesis (Matthew and Luke utilizing Mark and Q) that they will build entire edifices of interpretation upon it. While it is commonly accepted as a working hypothesis, few would wish to make it the core of redaction-critical research. Therefore, both in terms of tradition and source criticism, there is a degree of caution toward a full-blown redactional program.

Nevertheless, at a recent ETS (Evangelical Theological Society) meeting (1982) the basic approach was affirmed. The theological goals of redaction criticism parallel both rhetorical criticism (in the centrality of structure) and biblical theology (in the delineation of the individual author's message). Indeed, the basic desire to protect the author's intended meaning is best fulfilled by redaction criticism, which accents the final form over the separate traditions. For these reasons there is a growing affirmation of a nuanced methodology within evangelicalism. In similar fashion, a carefully controlled historical-critical method is strongly questioned but not negated, and the questions addressed to it are very similar to those asked by the broader spectrum of scholarship.

---

[79]   See Gerhard Maier, *The End of the Historical-Critical Method* (St. Louis: Concordia, 1977), and Gerhard Hasel, *Understanding the Living Word of God* (Mountain View, CA: Pacific Press, 1980).

E. Biblical Backgrounds.

Disciplines which uncover data bearing upon biblical history and customs have always been represented heavily in the evangelical school. The concern for the exact meaning of the text naturally leads to an emphasis upon the fields of archaeology, ancient languages, and history. At times there have been hasty conclusions drawn regarding the apologetic value of such finds as Jericho or the Hittites, and careful scholars now proclaim correctly that the primary value of archaeology is descriptive (providing data for understanding the biblical world) rather than apologetic (proving the historical reliability of accounts), since results are so tentative.[80] However, the value of such discoveries is immense, and our knowledge of the biblical world has increased dramatically in recent years.

There are several criteria for deciding when an extrabiblical parallel may be adduced in elucidating a text: (1) Do not assume that any thematic link constitutes a genealogical relationship. History-of-religions scholars have often assumed that Hellenistic parallels were superior to Jewish parallels; one must see which more closely elucidates the text. (2) Make certain that it comes from the same period; the mystery religions, for instance, stem from a later period and cannot be behind such New Testament practices as baptism. Also Talmudic evidence has often been used too casually without asking whether it truly stemmed from the pre-A.D. 70 Jewish situation. (3) Work not only with the current situation at the time of writing but also with the historical development behind it. Intertestamental allusions are critical for understanding the mindset of the New Testament writers. (4) Be holistic in your search. We can no longer assume that either Judaism or Hellenism is solely responsible for New Testament ideas, nor that Canaanite practices are responsible for Old Testament development. Recent studies have shown how cosmopolitan the ancient world actually was. (5) Look at wording and style. If the connection is no more than conceptual, it is possible but less likely than if one can denote an allusion to the parallel piece. (6) If differences outweigh similarities, one should consider other options. Preliminary theories regarding the influence of Qumran on the New Testament (e.g., with Jesus or John the Baptist) have been discarded because the similarities were overdrawn.

---

[80]   See Edwin Yamauchi, *The Stone and the Scriptures* (Philadelphia: Lippincott, 1972) 146-57.

Most importantly, historical background is deemed absolutely critical for a proper understanding of the text. The evangelical demand for propositional truth has always produced a great desire to determine the literal meaning of Scripture. This cannot be done adequately without applying the background behind the biblical statements, for one must recognize the analogical nature of biblical language and the cultural gap between it and our day. To overcome that gap, historical data is a critical need.

F. Semantics and Grammar.

Many evangelical schools still require Greek and Hebrew, and the biblical languages are deemed necessary for proper interpretation. The classical tenets of grammatical-syntactical exegesis are at the heart of the hermeneutical task. Students are required to study arduously the classical grammars such as Blass-Debrunner-Funk, Moulton-Hope-Turner, Zerwick and Moule for Greek, or Gesenius-Kautzsch, Hartmann, and Lambdin for Hebrew. Moreover, the cognate languages such as Akkadian, Sumerian, Ugaritic, and Aramaic are taught to those who wish to specialize. In fact, Trinity Evangelical Divinity School is one of the centers developing an exciting tool for grammatical research, called GRAMCORD, i.e., a Grammatical Concordance for the biblical languages employing computer programming. The grammatical configuration of the entire New Testament in Greek has been coded into the computer, and similar programs are in process for the Hebrew Old Testament as well as for the Septuagint and such extrabiblical literature as Josephus and Philo. Grammatical configurations can now be traced with precision and speed, and students in our advanced grammar course are already reworking major grammatical concepts. Judging from the growing number of SBL (Society of Biblical Literature) seminars and papers on this topic, this is clearly one of the major movements for the next decade.

Lexicography, the meaning of individual words and concepts, is also receiving new impetus in our day. The number of tools available for word studies has risen remarkably, and highly sophisticated studies along the lines of James Barr's classic *Semantics of Biblical Language* (1961) are readily available. In addition to the ten-volume *Theological Dictionary of the New Testament*, there is the well-written three-volume *New International Dictionary of New Testament Theology*, the three-volume *Exegetical Dictionary of the New Testament* (two volumes published as of this date), and many similar works. While to an extent many fall into Barr's criticism of "illegitimate totality transfer" (i.e., the tendency to read the whole theology behind a concept into individual uses of a term), there is evidence for a growing appreciation for proper lexical techniques (e.g, Silva's work in n. 14).

One major improvement lies in the use of parallels. In the past it has been common to read any possible parallel passage into the meaning of an individual statement. Thus there would be articles on the Essene background of the incarnational theology of Hebrews 2 alongside articles on the Hellenistic origin of that passage. Now there is a greater tendency to differentiate seeming parallels from true parallels. No longer can we interpret James' discussion of faith and works simply on the basis of Paul's teaching. Now we must examine the semantic linkage and the contextual meaning in both contexts before we establish connective lines between the two. I believe that the differences outweigh the similarities and that therefore we cannot establish a valid link between Paul and James.

The evangelical heritage, from A. T. Robertson and J. B. Lightfoot at the turn of the century to F. F. Bruce and I. Howard Marshall today, has always shown primary interest in this aspect of hermeneutics. The minutiae of the text have always had a particular fascination for evangelical preachers, as witness the number of years Martin Lloyd-Jones spent preaching on Romans or James Montgomery Boice on the Gospel of John. This of course is intimately connected to the view of Scripture, but it also is seen in the concomitant demand for accuracy, that is, the need to understand the parts before expounding the whole.

G. Biblical Theology and Systematic Theology.

The question of unity and diversity in the Bible has long fascinated scholars. Recently it has come to the fore in the debate on the validity of systematic theology. The Reformers stressed the principle of *analogia fidei*, the interpretation of individual portions of Scripture on the basis of other portions. Since the rise of the biblical theology movement in Germany in the eighteenth century, this principle has been under attack. The diverse emphases of individual portions of the Bible have so been stressed that any possibility of attaining a unified field of meaning which cuts across the differences has often been rejected as an impossible task. Theology, it is now being said, is descriptive rather than normative.

Evangelicals have always rejected this dichotomy as unnecessary (see Carson's article in n. 16). The basic unity is not a given, for it must be demonstrated. Diversity is certainly present between the documents. Yet this diversity does not rule out of hand the unity, and scholars argue that an interpreter can amalgamate individual statements into "covering models" which unify the diverse approaches to an issue into an overall biblical theology. Evangelicals would seek to maintain diversity (biblical theology) and yet to determine the underlying unity behind it (systematic theology). To stress the diversity at the expense of the unity is reductionistic; to stress the unity and ignore the diversity is speculative and subjective. When one goes beyond the surface language to the underlying concepts, the diverse statements are often seen to be compatible.

Nevertheless, one cannot ignore the surface meaning and "proof-text" dogma. It is also increasingly recognized that isolated biblical statements do not state dogmatic truths as much as apply aspects of the larger truth to circumstantial needs in the community addressed by the book. Dogma is determined by a complex process. First, one notes all the biblical passages which address a particular topic and exegetes those passages in terms of their original, intended meaning. Herein one notes tremendous diversity of emphasis and expression.

Next, the theologian begins the task of compilation. First, he or she elucidates the biblical theology of books and then authors on this topic. Second, one determines the larger unity within major traditions, e.g., the patriarchal/monarchical or prophetic periods in the Old Testament or the Palestinian or Gentile mission periods of the New Testament. Third, the full-fledged doctrine is traced through the biblical period, noting shifts of interest and the progress of revelation in salvation-history. This occurs under the aegis of biblical theology. Finally, the systematic theologian takes this data, seen in its diversity and unity, and restates it along the lines first of the history of dogma and second of the cultural expressions of the current age. In short, he or she reworks the biblical material so that it may be understood logically, in its whole and in its parts, by the modern person.

H. Contextualization.

We have moved from "what it meant" (the task of exegetical theology and biblical theology) to "what it means" (the task of systematic theology and homiletical theology). Contextualization, the hermeneutical side of homiletical theology, is the final step, linked with the task of proclamation. The theory has been developed by missiologists who are concerned for cross-cultural communication. Evangelicals, historically linked to pietistic and revivalist concerns, have always stressed this aspect. Contextualization says that the task of interpretation is never complete until one has wedded the exegesis of the Word to an exegesis of the world. The debate on this issue centers upon the interface between the two spheres. If the Word of God is propositional, one can "contextualize" the form but not the content of the biblical message. If it is functional (see n. 12), the current context would control the interpretation and one would develop an "indigenous theology" (the claim of the liberation theologian, for instance). The evangelical has always argued for the former stance.

The contextualization concerns the question of normative versus cultural interpretation. The interpreter asks whether the biblical command or principle is totally linked to the cultural situation (e.g., Paul's urban-centered evangelism at Ephesus in Acts 19) or whether the teaching transcends the circumstances and is normative for all ages (e.g., the Sermon on the Mount). For instance, this question is behind the widespread debate on the ordination of women in light of 1 Corinthians 14:34-36 and 1 Timothy 2:8-15. Some argue that the use of creation and the fall in these passages anchors the command to silence (not to teach) in God's redemptive decrees, and therefore it is meant for all ages. Others argue that the cultural background and the distance between the underlying principle (submission to husbands) and the command (not to teach) demonstrates a cultural rather than supracultural norm. The principle is that the supracultural content of Scripture is eternal/universal while cultural forms will apply the underlying principle differently depending upon the context.

Contextualization works with the results of the exegesis and cultural/supracultural delineation. It applies the biblical teaching to the receptor culture, and its purpose is to allow the Word to encounter the world. At times it will conform to current culture, and at other times it will confront modern man. In the latter sense, Scripture will challenge and then transform that culture. For the evangelical, it is important to note, this is not a subjective decision. The authority of the application varies in direct proportion to its conformity to the meaning of the text. Furthermore, the level of authority lessens as one moves away from the Scripture itself. Interpretation, since it is finite, has less authority than the text, and contextualization, another step away from interpretation, has even less authority. Therefore, for the evangelical, the process of interpretation-contextualization must remain tied to the propositional content of God's revelation. Again, it is the dynamic or functional aspect of biblical authority.

I.   Hermeneutics: A Summary.

It is important to realize that the evangelical principles elucidated above are quite distinct from the lines of authority elucidated by Harrington, Prokurat, and Burgess (in this volume). The Reformation principle of *sola scriptura* and the Scottish Common Sense Realism of the last century have produced an extremely eclectic situation. There is not the type of uniformity stemming from the Catholic principle of the magisterium. The sense of tradition is still true in evangelicalism, but it is under the surface of contemporary exposition and is restricted to denominational distinctives. This freedom has forced me to discuss constantly the different camps within evangelicalism on each of the issues above.

Above all, the importance of dialogue, or what I may call "community exegesis," must be stressed. It is through the interaction of the traditions that consensus is reached. This relates to the issue of separation discussed above and depends largely upon the evangelical willingness to dialogue with diverse traditions in order to arrive at "truth." For instance, while there is debate regarding the extent of inerrancy, there is consensus with respect to the propositional content of Scripture and the presence of both static and dynamic aspects of inspiration. The Bible deals with univocal truths expressed in analogical language, and so it is important to distinguish form from content. The exact details and significance of specific statements may differ, but the importance of the Bible for modern life is unilaterally accepted. As is the case with Catholicism, evangelicalism is tied more to the Church than to the academy. The issues of our day set the agenda for much of scholarly research, and it is strongly argued that the Bible must relate to modern life if it is to be relevant. The steps of interpretation as explicated above are all necessary to this task.

II. CASE STUDY—EPHESIANS 2:1-10

While the question of the authorship of Ephesians is not crucial to the interpretation of this book, most evangelicals would affirm that Paul has written it.[81] It is part of the group called the prison or captivity epistles (Ephesians, Philippians, Colossians, Philemon). Many believe that it was a circular letter, sent to Asia Minor, since *en Ephesô* is missing in many ancient manuscripts and it has the tone in places of a treatise. Thematically it centers upon an exalted Christology, that is, it presents the implications of the exalted Christ for the life of the Church, particularly for its unity and mission. As such, Ephesians focuses upon two aspects, the above and the below, the already and the not yet. In this sense, the crucial phrase is "in the heavenlies," that realm where the exalted Christ operates (1:20) and where we presently reign with him (2:6). At the same time it is the sphere of cosmic warfare (6:12), and God's activity in redemption makes the Church a living testimony to the cosmic forces of God's wisdom (3:10). Ephesians thus amalgamates the two spheres.

This tension is seen in chapters 1 to 3, which regulate God's activity in terms of his electing will (1:3-10) and the union of Jew and Gentile in the Church (1:11-14). Ephesians 2:1-10 occurs at the juncture between the power of God operative in the Church (1:19b-23) and the work of corporate salvation, centering upon the unity between Jew and Gentile, in 2:11-22. This paragraph describes the results of the divine salvific love upon those, Jew and Gentile alike, who were dead in sin.

The New International Version of the Bible, which was produced by an international group of Protestant scholars "committed to the full authority and complete trustworthiness of the Scriptures," translates Ephesians 2:1-10 as follows:

> [1]As for you, you were dead in your transgressions and sins, [2]in which you used to live when you followed the ways of this world and of the ruler of the kingdom of the air, the spirit who is now at work in those who are disobedient. [3]All of us also lived among them at one time, gratifying the cravings of our sinful nature and following its desires and thoughts. Like the rest, we were by nature objects of wrath. [4]But because of his great love for us, God, who is rich in mercy, [5]made us

---

[81]   See A. van Roon, *The Authenticity of Ephesians* (Leiden: E. J. Brill, 1974). For further data, see Andrew Lincoln's review article in *Westminster Theological Journal* 40 (1977-78) 172-75.

alive with Christ even when we were dead in transgressions—it is by grace you have been saved. [6]And God raised us up with Christ and seated us with him in the heavenly realms in Christ Jesus, [7]in order that in the coming ages he might show the incomparable riches of his grace, expressed in his kindness to us in Christ Jesus. [8]For it is by grace you have been saved, through faith—and this not from your- selves, it is the gift of God—[9]not by works, so that no one can boast. [10]For we are God's workmanship, created in Christ Jesus to do good works, which God prepared in advance for us to do.

The evangelical would first attempt a detailed grammatical and struc- tural analysis of the paragraph. In the original Greek, there are two sentences (vv. 1-7, 8-10), with the first sentence naturally comprising two sections (vv. 1-3, 4-7). Thus there is a tripartite structure, moving from the sinfulness of mankind (1-3) to the gracious provision of God in Christ (4-7) and concluding with a sweeping summary of this God- given salvation (8-10). The tone is clear: Sin is a result of influence from secular influences as well as hostile powers and results in rebellion, sensuality, and self-aggrandizement. The result is that all mankind is under the wrath of God.

Grammatically it is important to realize that the main verb for verse 1 does not appear until verse 5. As a result Paul keeps the reader in a state of tension as to the effects of "sin": Can it be overcome or not? The "then" and the "now" tension is clearly stressed,[82] for Paul continues his accent upon the individual believer's privileges.[83] The re- alized side of salvation is central, and the basis is the sovereign act of God. It is not on the basis of personal merit or "work" but solely by divine "grace." The terminology utilized to describe this mercy shows how incomprehensible it is to man. No single term can describe it. The God who has procured salvation on our behalf is "rich in mercy" ("rich" is found six times in Ephesians, more often than in any other New Testament book, and in Ephesians-Colossians it is always used of God)

---

[82]   For detailed discussions of the then-now schema, see Andrew Lincoln, *Ephesians* (WBC 42; Dallas:Word, 1990) 87-88.

[83]   For the corporate versus individual stress in Ephesians 1-2, see C. L. Mitton, *Ephesians* (New Century Bible, Greenwood, SC: Attic Press, 1976) 79-80. While he overdoes the individualistic aspect somewhat, he is basically correct that Paul here is looking at the individual within the Church.

and is characterized by "great love," a "grace" (twelve times in Ephesians!) which is "immeasurably rich," and by "kindness." All these reflect the Old Testament *hesed* the "lovingkindness" which is the basic relational attribute of God.

The sovereign control of God is clearly seen in the choice of language. It is God who has "made us alive"; we were "dead in transgressions" (v. 5, restating v. 1) and therefore could expect only divine "wrath" (v. 3). Salvation comes via "grace" (vv. 5b, 8a) and is the "gift of God" (v. 8c); it is "not via works," which would lead to "pride" (v. 9). It is clear that God alone distributes his salvific power; redemption cannot be claimed on the basis of human merit (for the Jew this specifically referred to legalistic righteousness; see Phil 3:9). In Ephesians 1-2, with a strong stress on God's electing will as the basis of Christian blessings, Paul wants the reader to understand perfectly that God, not man, is responsible for the basic privilege, salvation. It is clear in the context that "saved" (v. 8) is employed more narrowly of "justification" rather than broadly of the Christian life.

Yet the believer does have a part in the process. The "faith" response (v. 8) of the individual entails a complete openness or surrender of the self to God's salvific action. It is clear here that even this faith-response is not a work but itself is a "gift of God" (see Phil 1:29); it is "not of ourselves" but is possible only because of the enabling power of God.[84] At the same time it is important to realize that Paul is not bypassing human choice, i.e., free will. Of course there are many different formulations of this debate, from Augustine versus Pelagius in the fifth century to the Calvinist versus Arminian controversies of our own time. Whatever one's perspective (and I confess that I am nearer to Arminianism on this issue), it is crucial here to preserve both sovereignty and free will in the formula.

Moreover, I would stress the importance of community exegesis here. The interpreter must be in constant dialogue with the past community of faith (the history of dogma) and the current community of faith (recent commentaries, etc.) on this point as well as others.

The present and future results of this congruence between divine grace and human faith in salvation are also highlighted in 2:1-10. These

---

[84]   See the fine discussion of this point in Markus Barth, *Ephesians* (Anchor Bible; Garden City, NY: Doubleday, 1974) 224-25. He points to the conjunction here of God's (and Christ's) faithfulness with our faith.

are found in verses 5-7, 10. First, the believer has been "made alive" or "raised up" (from spiritual death—v. 5a). For Paul the birth of faith is the hour of resurrection (see Rom 6:8; Gal 2:16, 20; Col 2:12; 3:1) and leads to "newness of life" (Rom 6:6; 2 Cor 5:17-20; Eph 4:22-24; Col 3:8-10). Second, God has "made (the believer) sit in the heavenlies with Christ," a remarkable passage in that it adds to Jesus' exaltation in 1:20 the Christian's exaltation here. The believer shares not only Christ's resurrection but also his exaltation. Yet, as Lincoln says, "The phrase ... 'at his right hand' in 1:20 is reserved for Christ and not repeated in the case of believers in 2:6. Although believers share in Christ's exaltation, his position in the heavenly realm and his relationship to God are unique."[85] It is important to note the past tense, which indicates that this eschatological exaltation is not a future promise but a present reality, based undoubtedly on the Pauline metaphor of adoption. Due to God's gracious inclusion of us in his family, we are "joint-heirs" (Rom 8:15-17) and thus share Jesus' exalted status.

The final present blessing is found in verse 10, which describes our "creation" as God's "workmanship" in order that we might perform "good works." This is important as a clarification of the common belief that Paul and James are at odds on faith and works. A semantic mapwork of their use of terms indicates their basic agreement: A professed (but false) faith (James) which seeks works-righteousness (Paul) is useless (Paul and James); only a true faith (Paul) which leads to good works (James and Paul here in 2:10) is valid. The concept of faith put to work in acts of charity is central in the pastoral epistles, where "good works" appears eight times.

The future aspect is found in verse 7 and is important for the already/not yet tension in Ephesians (see above). While there is debate as to whether the "coming ages" means future generations of Christians or the eschaton, it is likely that no either-or response is possible. Both are probably in mind. The "immeasurable riches" manifested in his "kindness toward us" will be experienced by all future ages of the Church and will be consummated in the second coming of Christ.

The contextualization (or "transfer value," to use Harrington's phrase) of this passage is very direct for the evangelical. Meditation upon one's past state in sin is integral to the meaning of salvation. The three characteristics of verses 2-3 (rebellion, sensuality, self-centeredness)

---

85   Lincoln, *Ephesians*, 107.

describe the common dilemma of man, as demonstrated in recent sociological and psychological profiles of men and women in this modern postindustrial society. This, we would argue, is true of both secular man and those who now belong to the Church.[86]

The distinction between conversion language and maintenance language posed by Harrington makes a great deal of sense here. Yet at the same time I doubt whether Paul would strongly emphasize the difference. The aorist (past) tenses of the verbs ("made alive," "raised up," "made to sit") must be seen in the light of the perfect periphrastic "have been saved," which stresses the present condition. Paul actually is stressing the present Christian situation of resurrection life which has resulted from the past conversion. Once again, it is not an either-or. For this reason, the dynamic power, the exalted status, and the concomitant demand for good works are eminently applicable. Finally, the evangelical endorses the necessity of conversion language for our day. The depravity of man, the salvific sacrifice of Christ, and the indispensability of faith-decision are at the heart of the revivalist spirit so endemic to the movement.

III. SUMMARY

Evangelicals have always made a "high" view of biblical authority a basic tenet of their faith. In spite of the widespread debate today over the exact formulation of such issues as "inerrancy," evangelicals consistently stress that Scripture alone must dictate our faith. While there is cognizance of the complex nature of the interpretive task and the factor of preunderstanding as shaping that interpretation, there is unanimity that the intention of the author is both a possible goal and a necessary element in determining the meaning of the Bible in our day. At the same time, the relevant significance of Scripture is also stressed, and the interdependence between exegesis, biblical theology, historical theology, systematic theology, and contextualization forms the core of evangelical hermeneutics.

The grammatical-historical method predominates. The tools of textual and source criticism, syntactical (grammar) and semantic (word)

---

[86] Here the application depends upon one's view of the sacrament of baptism. Most evangelicals, even from a strongly sacramental position, would argue that a later faith-discussion parallel to that in this passage must occur.

study, and form, redaction, and narrative criticisms are all subordinate to the task of elucidating the text. After several decades of isolation, there is a growing desire once again to engage in dialogue with other traditions, and indeed this book is an important part of that movement. An "evangelical" reading of Ephesians 2:1-10 stresses the Pauline origin of the teaching and its connection with Romans 1-8 and related texts. The progress of the passage fits the dilemma of modern humanity, locked in sin and needing to apply the salvific grace of God and the sacrifice of Christ in a conversion experience. Divine grace and human faith meet in the supreme gift of faith-decision. This unlocks God's workmanship inherent in man/woman, leading to the "good works" which characterize the presence of God in the community.

RECOMMENDED READINGS

Black, David Alan and David S. Dockery, eds. *New Testament Criticism and Interpretation*. Grand Rapids: Zondervan, 1991. An excellent series of articles on critical methods such as text and source criticism and schools such as form, redaction, and literary criticism.

Carson, D. A. and John Woodbridge, eds. *Scripture and Truth*. Grand Rapids: Zondervan, 1983. A series of essays centering upon the importance of inerrancy and a propositional approach to Scripture.

_____. *Hermeneutics, Authority, and Canon*. Grand Rapids: Zondervan, 1986. A second series of articles similar to the 1983 volume.

Fee, Gordon and Douglas Stuart. *How to Read the Bible for All Its Worth*. Philadelphia: Westminster, 1982. An excellent general discussion on the proper approach to specfic genres, e.g., poetry, wisdom, gospels, Acts.

Hatch, Nathan O. and Mark A. Noll, eds. *The Bible in America: Essays in Cultural History*. New York: Oxford University Press, 1982. A series of essays tracing the progress of interpretation in various traditions in American Christianity.

Klein, William, Craig L. Blomberg, and Robert L. Hubbard, Jr. *Introduction to Biblical Interpretation*. Dallas: Word, 1993. An excellent, up-to-date introduction to hermeneutics from an evangelical perspective.

Marsden, George B. *Fundamentalism and American Culture: The Shaping of Twentieth Century Evangelicalism 1870-1925*. New York: Oxford University Press, 1980. A major work on the factors which led to the fundamentalist/evangelical movement.

Marshall, I. Howard, ed. *New Testament Interpretation: Essays on Principles and Methods*. Grand Rapids: Eerdmans, 1977. Essays tracing various schools and issues in the field of hermeneutics, demonstrating the many differences in the approaches of evangelicals as they interact with diverse critical issues.

Nicole, Roger R. and J. Ramsey Michaels, eds. *Inerrancy and Common Sense*. Grand Rapids: Baker, 1980. Essays tracing various aspects, both academic and practical, on the issue of biblical authority. More than other works on inerrancy, this demonstrates the various evangelical approaches.

Osborne, Grant R. *The Hermeneutical Spiral: A Comprehensive Introduction of Biblical Interpretation*. Downer's Grove, IL: InterVarsity Press, 1991. An attempt to integrate every aspect (exegesis, biblical and systematic theology, contextualization) of hermeneutical inquiry into a comprehensive whole.

Rogers, Jack and Donald McKim. *Authority and Interpretation of the Bible: An Historical Approach*. New York: Harper and Row, 1979. An attempt to show that a more dynamic model of biblical authority existed from the patristic period until the Princetonians of the last century.

Silva, Moises. *Biblical Words and Their Meaning: An Introduction to Lexical Semantics*. Grand Rapids: Zondervan, 1983. Not only a study of the methods of lexical study but also an illustration of the implications of a propositional approach to Scripture.

Tate, W. R. *Biblical Interpretation*. Peabody, MA: Hendrickson, 1991. Provides good discussion of cultural issues in hermeneutics like author and reader or the interpretive schools.

Thiselton, Anthony C. *The Two Horizons: New Testament Hermeneutics and Philosophical Description*. Grand Rapids: Eerdmans, 1980. A major discussion of the hermeneutical problem of the past (what it meant) and present (what it means) problem in interpretation theory, using the approaches of Heidegger, Bultmann, and Gadamer as the control.

_____. *New Horizons in Hermeneutics: The Theory and Practice of Transforming Biblical Reading*. Grand Rapids: Zondervan, 1992. An unbelievably comprehensive interaction with every modern school of hermeneutical thought. Difficult, yet must reading for the serious student.

Woodbridge, John D. *Biblical Authority: A Critique of the Rogers/McKim Proposal*. Grand Rapids: Zondervan, 1982. Argues contra Rogers and McKim (above) that the Church down through the ages held a view of propositional authority or total infallibility

SCRIPTURE AS WORD OF GOD AND THE
ECUMENICAL TASK
by
George H. Tavard, A.A.

The intent of this essay is to examine a question that has been implicitly at the center of debates between Catholics and Protestants, both in the polemical times of the Reformation and Counter Reformation and in the ecumenical dialogues of the twentieth century. What do we affirm when we designate Scripture as the Word of God? I am not asking about what various theologians have understood by the expression; nor am I concerned with varieties of interpretation, but with essential statement. In addition, my concern is not with specific theologies but with the Church and its organic tradition as a whole. The ecclesial context shapes the approach of theologians and of the educated faithful, at least in their main lines, as they interpret, spontaneously or reflexively, what Scripture says. In this ecclesial context I wish to deal more specifically with what meaning the Catholic tradition has given to the assertion that Scripture is the Word of God.

The question is of importance for the structure of dialogue, which, as Pope Paul VI affirmed in his encyclical *Ecclesiam suam* (in 1964, the third year of Vatican II), belongs to the essence of the Church. The multifaceted dialogue in which the Christian world is now engaged is first of all internal, as between Oriental Orthodox, Byzantine Orthodox, Catholics, and Protestants, and also, less markedly, classical Pentecostal and fundamentalist churches. It is also increasingly external, that is, with other religions, several of which also have Scriptures that they regard as being in some sense Word of God.

I. ECCLESIAL CONTEXT

The ecclesial context of catholicity may be looked at from two angles. Synchronically, this context is the Catholic communion as it now lives under the primacy of Pope John Paul II, in the puzzling circumstances of the postconciliar period, the coming end of the twentieth century, the ensuing dawn of the third millennium after Christ, and the turmoil and uncertainty that are following the breakup of the Soviet Union, the disappearance of Communist dictatorships in Eastern Europe, and their resilience in Asia. Diachronically, this context is the Catholic tradition. Historians of religious ideas and institutions can compare it with parallel traditions in other Christian communions, and even with corresponding, if not parallel, traditions in some of the other great world religions. This tradition has had an undeniable continuity through time even if it has undergone certain shifts and turns. This continuity has given the Catholic reality a recognizable consistency, a sort of thickness that may need to be peeled off if we are to grasp the heart of the Catholic reading of Scripture as Word of God.

Catholic theology and practice, however, have also conveyed the impression that the normativity of Scripture has been qualified in Catholic context, not only by reference to a normativity of tradition, but also by obedience to the authority that has been recognized to, or assumed by, the living magisterium of bishops. This was of course the main reason why the normativity of the Word of God was pointedly underlined by the Reformers in their appeal to Scripture alone.

II. TRADITION

The Catholic ethos has indeed given particular importance to the weight of tradition. The present moment is never seen apart from its origination in the past. The contemporary coordinates of a doctrine, teaching, institution, or practice are never sufficient to explain it. One also needs to trace its roots. Searching the ground of contemporary doctrine, the Catholic division of history has pinpointed certain moments, chiefly those of ecumenical councils, as being normative for the present. To the critical observer it would then seem that the present church bows to selected episodes in the past. To the believer, critical or naive, it means that the Church lives from memory, and that this memory, like all memories, has been selective. If it is healthy, the Church's memory selects those events that have born the clearest witness, given their time and place, to the original memory that lies at the very heart of the Christian consciousness, namely, the memory of the Lord.

Indeed, Christian churches differ at the level of these remembered events. They do not remember the Reformation or the Council of Trent in the same way. Yet they also differ at the very level of the original memory, if at least some of them identify the centrally remembered event as the Last Supper, others as the crucifixion, and others perhaps as the resurrection. Each of these remembered moments is then haloed with a unique theological emphasis: the Last Supper evokes the real presence of the Lord among his people on earth; the cross of Jesus underlines gratuitous salvation; the resurrection highlights the present anticipation of eschatological transformation. Into their central memory of the presence, Catholics have also, and more than ever since the end of the nineteenth century, inserted the sound of the living magisterial voice, both that of bishops at large and the increasingly strident voice of the bishop of Rome in the exercise of what is believed to be the continuing ministry of the first of the apostles.

Authority for the Catholic mind has thus been not only that of the Word of God in Scripture; it has also been that of the tradition. Or, in the more recent formulation that was endorsed, perhaps too hastily, by Vatican II, it has been the authority of the tradition and of the magisterium. I say, hastily, because if the magisterium is no longer seen as part of the tradition but as an additional source of authority that is connumerated with Scripture and the tradition, its seeming importance hides the fact that it has lost its foundation that can lie nowhere else than in Scripture and in tradition. Yet, whether one counts two or three points of reference in the Catholic pattern of authority, one cannot assume that the relationships between the two or the three are never conflictual. Historians have told the story of periods of crisis when conflicts surfaced. In order to illustrate the question, we will need to look briefly at what the councils of Trent and of Vatican II said about tradition.

III. TIME AND TRADITION

There is, it would seem, a preliminary question in regard to tradition. The recognition that tradition is a major ingredient in the Christian self-definition throws light on a problem that has been seldom addressed in modern theology, the problem of the nature of time.

St. Augustine examined this question at length in the Confessions. That time held a prominent place in Augustine's reflection about the process of his conversion is often disconcerting to readers of the Confessions who are chiefly looking for edification. This is easily understandable since catechetical practice has frequently separated scholarly knowledge and piety. As I will point out further below, the Catechism of the Catholic church, published by virtue of the apostolic constitution *Fidei depositum* (October 11, 1992), is not exempt from this failing.

By contrast, the early reflection of the bishop of Hippo turned
around the ways of divine grace. As he looked over the course of his
life from his infancy through his years in Italy to his return home to
Africa, Augustine could see that God had mysteriously led him from a
practical paganism through the doctrines of the Manichees to the books
Cicero and of Neo-Platonists to the epistles of Paul. He had been led,
slowly and painfully, to the faith that the Logos of God, the Verbum
that is second in the eternal Trinity, had truly become man, sharing
temporal existence with us as Jesus of Nazareth. What then can it mean
that the Eternal has lived temporally? The theological answer of the
Greeks, that had been effectively used against the doctrines of Arius,
pointed out that the Logos has been made flesh so that his followers
may be in some sense deified. The divine Word shared temporality so
that those who are by nature temporal could share eternity by grace.
This of course was not to be denied in the context of Latin theology.
But it was an appeal to mystery. The Greek mind could be familiar
with this: One does not understand a mystery by dialectics but by
participation, as it were from the inside; one enters it by faith.

This, however, posed serious philosophical questions to the dialec-
tical mind of the Latin rhetorician that Augustine still was in his early
years as bishop of Hippo. He therefore devoted considerable attention,
not to mystery as such, but to the nature of time in Book XI of the
Confessions. Time is compared to the slow flow of water falling drop
by drop, presumably on the model of the water clocks that existed at
the period or on that of an hourglass in which grains fall through a
narrow neck, marking the passage of time. "The drops of time are dear
to me,"[87] Augustine declares. Why? Because each one of them can and
should be devoted to the praise and glory of God. Thus the passage of
time, disconcerting as it may be when one feels the marks of aging in
one's own body or when one observes the instability of civilizations
that go through periods of decay after promising periods of rise, is also
the providential offer of moments of praise for the Creator. For, Augustine asks himself, how is the passing of time lived? The common
language refers to time past, present, and future. But this is illusionary.
In reality there is only the present, but this present is itself successive:
"There are three things in the soul, and I do not see them anywhere

<hr>

[87]   Confessions, XI, ii, 2; see my volume, Les jardins de saint Augustin. Lecture des "confessions" (Montreal: Bellarmine, 1988) 18-22.

else: the present memory of things past, the present attention to things present, and the present expectation of things future."[88] One may conclude from this that "there are three times: the present of what is past, the present of what is present, and the present of what is future."

Now, as he reflected on the nature of time Augustine was raising the more immediately theological question of the nature of tradition. He did not, I believe, realize this as he wrote the Confessions, for the simple reason that he was not yet sufficiently involved in the theological controversies that were to occupy much of his life, on revelation (against the Manicheans), on grace (against Pelagius and his followers), on the sacraments and the Church (against the Donatists). As was made evident in these controversies, neither the meaning of Scripture nor the determination of doctrine was ensured once for all with the adoption of the biblical canon and the acknowledgement of the faith that was formulated at Nicaea. The necessity to call councils and synods, in some of which Augustine himself was to take part, as at the anti-Pelagian synod of Carthage in 416, illustrated the fact that as the life of the Church flows on it follows a time of its own.

Ecclesial time is not identical with generic time. Nor does it coincide with imperial or political time. That is, the transmission of true doctrine in fidelity to the Scriptures is not a mere succession of teaching. Teaching undergoes successive but not homogeneous phases, that are marked by the discussion of hypotheses, the raising of questions, the adoption of wrong solutions, the emergence of false doctrines, their denunciations as heresies, the conciliar determination of true doctrine. The difficulty of deciding what is correct teaching of the faith, true praise of God, faithful acknowledgement of the Word at work in creation and of the Spirit at work in the Church and in Christian life illustrates what the later Augustine will diagnose as the coexistence of the City of God, *civitas sanctorum*, that is based on love of God going to contempt of self, with the city of evil, that is based on love of self going to contempt of God, and the practical impossibility of sorting them out in the concrete reality of the *ecclesia* in its temporal existence. Thus the time of the Church, ecclesial time, is identical with the tradition of doctrine. And this is not, except in an idealizing oversimplification of facts, a harmonious succession of teaching "from parent

---

[88]   *Confessions*, XI, xx, 26.

to child."[89] It is a recurring struggle of good and evil as these affect the soul and the mind, and thereby the selection and formulation of what is taught and believed.

The succession of teaching (giving, passing on) and believing (receiving), and then teaching again, and so on indefinitely, is not exempt from the ambiguity of time. For the experience of the present necessarily colors both one's memory of the past and one's anticipation of the future. The Christian as individual believer and the Church as the local and universal congregation of the faithful are affected by the same kind of ambiguity. Neither the believer nor the collectivity is infallibly protected from the equivocities of temporal existence. The mark of sinfulness, which Augustine detected in the *massa perditionis* of humanity, is bound to affect the church militant as long as Christ has not yet withdrawn it from the temporalities of the world, as long as it does not fully coincide with the church triumphant in heaven, as long as the City of Men is not isotopic with the City of the Saints that is the eternal City of God. Even the predestined, in Augustine's theology, do not know that they are predestined and must go on struggling with ambiguity.

What does this mean regarding the nature of ecclesial time? One may take a cue from the language of late medieval theology and the Council of Trent as it spoke of Scripture and the apostolic traditions. They did not, as was seen earlier, personalize tradition in the singular as one reality next to Scripture. That they saw it as traditions in the plural implies that what the Counter Reformation construed as a unified *traditio,* as one uniform or continuous stream of transmission of doctrine or of the interpretation of Scripture, protected from error (with Vatican I and II, by the ecclesial, conciliar, and papal charism of infallibility that ensures the formulation of irreformable doctrines), was previously perceived as a discontinuous series of moments, drops of the flow of time, in which the face of the past moves is reshaped and repainted by the convictions of the present, and the hoped for perfection to come varies with the lacks, wishes, and projects of the present.

In this perspective, the Augustinian meditation on the nature of time introduces a principle of uncertainty in the tradition. In the threefold reference of time to the past, the present, and the future, there is a

---

[89]   See my *The Seventeenth-Century Tradition. A Study in Recusant Thought* (Leiden: E. J. Brill, 1978) 188-89.

necessary priority of the present. For it is in the present that one re-
members and mentally reconstructs the past and that one looks forward
to the future and to the fulfillment of the promises that have been read
in the past and that are sensed in the present. Likewise it is always in
the light of the present that Scripture is read, preached, taught, and
interpreted. And it is in the same light of the present and in that of the
past that has been thus reinterpreted that one hopes for the future,
whether this is the twenty-first century and the third millennium or
the eschaton. Thus the Church's self-awareness in the present holds the
key to its memory and mental reconstruction of the past, to its reading, preaching, teaching, and interpreting of Scripture, to its formulation
of faith, and to its promise and tentative construction of the future.

But in this case what the late Carl Peter liked to call the Catholic
principle[90]—namely the notion that the grace of God is so embodied in
the earthly reality of the *Ecclesia* that it brings to Christian life and
doctrine an element of absolute and total confidence—cannot be accepted without considerable qualification. If indeed the subjective
element in the Augustinian analysis of time is in fact at work at the
very heart of the tradition, then there is nothing in the tradition that is
given to us as a pure and totally objective datum. It all needs to be sifted
through faith which, being objectively true in Christ, is subjectively
received and personally assimilated. At this point the analysis of time
as applied to the ecclesial time that flows through the Church's tradition converges on Luther's insight that justification, which is totally
God's gift in Christ alone, is in us through faith, which is itself totally
God's gift in the Holy Spirit. Every ecclesial doctrine and institution
needs to be sifted through it.

I would therefore not put Scripture and tradition side by side or
face to face, even in an existential dialectic as in Paul Tillich's too neat
dichotomy of Protestant principle and Catholic substance. But I would
recognize a fact that is at the heart of the tradition understood in its
modern identification with the total life of the Church, liturgical, doctrinal, and moral. The tradition that has been inherited in the Church
from past ages includes bad liturgy as well as good, false doctrine as
well as true, sinfulness as well as virtuousness. Ultimately it is not the

---

[90]   H. George Anderson, T. Austin Murphy, and Joseph A. Burgess, eds.
    Justification by Faith. Lutherans and Catholics in Dialogue VII (Minne-
    apolis: Augsburg, 1985) 304-15.

tradition of received doctrines that provides the certainty of faith, whether defined in its subjective strength or in its objective identification of belief. The certainty of faith can only derive—not from a tentative reconstruction of the past, from a transmission of what has been remembered, and still less from the numerous traditions that have contributed to the church's history—but from the Word who may at times, discontinuously, be heard through the multiplicity of human words that are spoken in the Church and read in the Scriptures, and from the Spirit who makes the Word speak and live in the heart of the faithful as these are made aware of being justified by faith alone in Christ alone.

The question of the nature of time was still examined by the Scholastics in the context of the theology of creation, specifically of the creation of matter (time properly so called, in commentaries on the *Sentences*, Book II, Distinction I) and of the creation of angels (*aevum*, or angelic duration, in Distinction II). In more recent centuries, however, the question has commonly been left out of the theological field of vision, along with a general lack of interest in a theology of creation and of nature. The question of the nature of time is then abandoned to philosophers, such as Heidegger[91] and Jean Paul Sartre.[92] Since Einstein and the theory of generalized relativity, time can also be identified as a scientific problem. It has thus become a natural phenomenon that can be investigated by the sciences of nature and, as with Stephen Hawking, by advanced physics and mathematics.[93]

Theology, however, needs to claim it back, that is, to recover the sense that it holds a unique key to understand the nature of time. The question of time belongs directly to the investigation of Holy Scripture. For, as was noted by Augustine in a passage that is quoted in the *Catechism of the Catholic Church*, the incarnation required the submission to time of One who lives out of time: "Remember that one Word of God is spread out through all the Scriptures, that One Word re-

91   *Being and Time* (New York: Harper & Row, 1962); original German, *Sein und Zeit* (Tübingen: Neomarius Verlag, 1927).

92   *L'Etre et le néant. Essai d'ontologie phénoménologique* (Paris: Gallimard, 1943).

93   Stphen Hawking, *A Brief History of Time. From the Big Bang to Black Holes* (New York: Bantam Books, 1988).

sounds in the mouth of the sacred writers, the One who, being at the beginning with God, has no need of syllables there because there he is not subject to time."[94] In contrast, the subjection of the divine Word to time as Jesus of Nazareth entailed his speaking in the broken language of humanity and the writing of the Scriptures as the primary embodiment of this speaking. Likewise it is because of the nature of time that the divine revelation given in Christ reaches distinct generations of believers in their own times and places through the transmission or tradition of the faith.

IV. The Council of Trent

The decree that was promulgated at the Council of Trent on the 8th of April, 1546, was short. But agreement about its meaning and scope has been long to come. Strictly speaking, the decree did not bear on Scripture as such, but on the foundation on which the council wished to base its future decisions. In the Tridentine language, these would be based on the gospel, and the gospel would be known through Scripture and the traditions.

Scripture was identified as the books of the Old Testament Septuagint along with those of the New Testament, both of which were then familiar to the West chiefly in their rendering in the Latin Vulgate. But there was little concern regarding the interpretation and use of Scripture. On the one hand this question was not faced as such in the decree. On the other hand, an element of ambiguity was introduced by the way Scripture was joined to the traditions.

The traditions in question were understood to be those teachings that formulate doctrine (not discipline) and that also have been transmitted from the apostles down to our day (and therefore not traditions of more recent origin). In context, the apostles were the twelve apostles mentioned in the New Testament, plus of course St. Paul. But it is agreed today that the group of apostles was broader and must include the other missionaries who, like Paul, brought the gospel to the nations. In light of modern views of history, however, the traditions thus identified do not constitute a sufficient and comprehensive tool for the establishment of doctrine. For it is practically impossible to ascertain

---

94 *Catéchisme de l'Eglise catholique.* (Paris: Mame/Plon), n. 102, p. 35, from *Enarr. In Ps.* 103, 4, 1.

the apostolicity of specific doctrines. What goes back to the apostles themselves is a moot point.

Scripture and the apostolic traditions are joined in the Tridentine decree by the word, *et*, "and." Many questions were raised in the 1950s about the implications of this copula. Are the traditions placed on an equal basis with Scripture? Are the two connumerated as independent and parallel sources of Christian doctrine? Is one of them subordinated to the other? Are they mutually implied in each other? Are they complementary in their contents, or only in their tone and their approach to doctrine? Is each one complete without the other? Or are the traditions no more than historical channels through which Scripture has been transmitted from age to age? What did Trent mean with its statement that it regards Scripture and the apostolic traditions *pari pietatis affectu ac reverentia*, "with an equal affection of piety and veneration"?

These and related questions were debated in Catholic theology shortly before Vatican II. According to the conclusion that I myself reached at the time,[95] Trent believed that the meaning of Scripture emerges in the apostolic traditions. In the language of "word and sacrament," dear to the Reformers, the meaning of the written word is elicited by faithful practice of the sacraments, for the sacraments themselves draw their graceful contents from the promise of Christ that is conveyed in the word, this promise being called, in classical Catholic language, their divine institution. Thus, in the Tridentine formulation, Scripture and the traditions deserve "one and the same affection of piety" because they are inseparable. In the message of Scripture the traditions find their ultimate origin and justification; and it is through the traditions that the message of Scripture is carried to the postapostolic generations. The Church's teaching and belief as they are being lived unfold the meaning of Scripture in the hearts of the faithful.

V. VATICAN COUNCIL II

The discussions of the 1950s about the decree of Trent remotely paved the way for the constitution *Dei Verbum* of Vatican II (November 18, 1965). In contrast with the Tridentine emphasis on the gospel, attention was then focused on revelation. It is the divine revelation that is written in Scripture and transmitted by tradition (now usually con-

---

[95]   *Holy Writ or Holy Church. The Crisis of the Protestant Reformation* (New York: Harper, 1959) 207-09.

ceptualized in the singular). As to the meaning of Scripture, it is approached from two different angles.

From a "material" point of view, Vatican II equates this meaning with "what the sacred writers truly meant and God gracefully revealed through their words" (ch. 3, no. 12). Two principles should be at work in the process of uncovering this meaning. First, one should take account of the "literary forms" and the "customary, indigenous ways of feeling, of speaking, or of telling a tale that obtained in the sacred authors' times, and of those commonly used in human relations at that period." Second, "Scripture must be read and interpreted in the same spirit in which it was written." One can also read this sentence in the masculine: "in the same Spirit in whom it was written." In either case the Holy Spirit is at work, whether directly or in the effects of divine inspiration. But how are we to identify the sense of the Spirit? *Dei Verbum* suggests a triple criterion: the coherence of the whole Scripture, harmony with the Church's living tradition, and the analogy of faith. But the living tradition will not be complete before this world ends and the New Jerusalem is made manifest. In other words, the full meaning of Scripture will be an eschatological event, what the council calls "the wondrous descent of eternal Wisdom to our level" (no. 13). Before the eschaton, the nearest approximation of this Wisdom is no other than the sum total of the living tradition until our own time, the Church of the past and the present seen and experienced as one, in anticipation of the eschatological fulfillment.

A second point of view, that one may call "final," is thus introduced, which is developed in the last chapter of *Dei Verbum:* The written Word of God is not given only for the sake of the objective truth of its contents as divine revelation but also for the purpose of nurturing the life of the faithful, for its value as spiritual nourishment. To believers it should be "strength of their faith, food for their soul, pure and perennial font of their spiritual life" (no. 21). Word and sacrament are then joined together, for the eucharistic table is "both that of the Word of God and that of the body of Christ." Word and sacrament, the text affirms, have always been considered by the Church "along with Holy Tradition, as the supreme rule of her faith." In turn, "theology rests upon the written Word of God in unity with Holy Tradition" (no. 24). This is the source of all ministry.

The doctrine of Vatican II may then be summed up in the idea that Scripture has a twofold relevance: to the formulation of doctrine, insofar as it depicts the earliest reception of the revelation to the apostles; and to the growth of faith, that is inspired and illustrated by it as a God-given parable of the believers' experience of grace.

VI. PATRISTIC ORIGINS

The doctrine of Scripture as Word of God belongs to a long theological tradition. In the first centuries the Fathers of the church, the Greeks first, followed and echoed by the Latins, viewed only the Old Testament as Scripture, which witnessed to the future coming of the Lord, the Living Word. When Christ came as its fulfillment, no other Scriptures were, in principle, needed. The incarnate Word was himself known from the "rule of faith" (*regula fidei*), which may be practically identified with the baptismal creed, the contents of which were supported by the apostolic writings. But in the controversies against the Gnostics and against Marcion these apostolic writings were recognized as, or, if one prefers, promoted to the rank of, Scripture; and since they differ from the previous Bible in that they speak directly and explicitly of Christ, they quickly became the primary Scriptures of Christians. Once the accretion of the New Testament to the Scriptures was finalized, the christocentric interpretation of all Scripture, Old and New, became more marked, and Scripture gained a priority of its own as that element in the tradition that reveals the ways of the divine Word on earth.

As is patent to any reader of homiletic literature, however, Scripture soon acquired, especially among the later fathers, a multitude of senses. Already for Origen the historical or literal sense served as starting point for spiritual applications. Scripture is the food of the soul. And if the Christian soul lives by faith, this faith is nurtured by the experience of Christian love and by the imagination which projects the present into the eschatological future and anticipates the eschatological future in the present—which is the core of the Christian hope. In its early stages, the investigation of spiritual senses may have been indebted to the hermeneutics of Philo and to the ways of Hellenistic rhetoric. But it was soon channeled into three privileged senses that were connected with faith, love, and hope. In his *Moralia in Job* Gregory the Great was less interested in the literal textual sense than in its relevance to these three aspects of Christian life.

VII. THE MEDIEVAL EPISODE

In its monastic flowering from the eighth to the twelfth century, the medieval tradition shared the patristic concern about the threefold application of Scripture. Yet with the end of the twelfth century and the blossoming of scholastic theology in the thirteenth, systematic thought increasingly shaped the interpretation of Scripture and the identification of its meaning or meanings. Where rhetoric formerly acted as the chief ancillary support of biblical hermeneutics, grammar first, then logic, and finally metaphysics acquired status as tools for scriptural interpretation. In the process, however, meaning changed. It came to be more closely related to the recipients of the Word. Thus, innumerable medieval authors found the sense of Scripture in the Church seen metaphorically as the universal bride of Christ, in the souls of the faithful as Christ's individual brides, and in the Virgin Mary as the typical, iconic bride in whom both the Church and the soul are given a graceful model. Faith, love, and hope—each of them a gift of God, but a gift that comes alive in the believer's human conscience—determined the chief variants of spiritual interpretation, namely, the analogical, tropological, and anagogical senses.

The basic process was neatly summed up by Hugh of St. Victor, who, in the twelfth century, was deeply concerned about Christian symbols:

> The exposition [of Scripture] contains three points, the letter, the sense, the *sententia* [doctrine]. The letter is the proper ordering of discourse. The sense is the easy and obvious signification that the letter presents at face-value. The *sententia* is the deeper understanding that cannot be found without exposition and interpretation.... First the letter, then the sense, then the *sententia:* when this is done the explanation is finished.[96]

In this general framework a number of authors—such as the Cistercian abbot, Baldwin of Canterbury, and the Franciscan Bonaventure—made it clear that the literal sense of the New Testament is already spiritual. It is the letter itself, *littera*, and not the reader's imagination, that is the locus of the spiritual senses, that implies both *sensus* and *sententia*. What is to be believed, what is to be done, what is to be hoped for are no other than what the letter says as it speaks of the person, the words, and the actions of Christ. In this case spiritual dimensions are not added to the letter. But the letter is itself fully spiritual.

---

[96] *Didascalion,* Ii, 9.

It opens windows on the basic dimensions of faith which the Scholastics itemized, in light of their faculty psychology, as the theological virtues of faith, love, and hope. As to the letter of the Old Testament, it finds its spiritual meaning, as Bonaventure explained, not in itself but in the New, for Abraham, Moses, and the prophets said and did nothing that did not eventually refer to Christ.

The prophecy of Joachim of Fiora was not entirely alien to this logic, when, pushing the process further, the Calabrian abbot affirmed that the meaning of the New Testament is not the last that is intended by God. An eschatological meaning is still to be revealed, a mystery to be unfolded. What the church did not accept in the thirteenth century (Lateran Council IV, 1215) was Joachim's notion that this unfolding will lead to a new revelation of the Spirit in a purely monastic *ecclesia*, beyond Christ and the present form of the Church.

Martin Luther himself stood squarely in the line of monastic theology and the basic medieval tradition when, without abandoning the vocabulary of the spiritual sense, he focused the reading of the Bible on "what carries Christ" (*was Christum treibet*), what the letter of Scripture says of Christ's saving work that is effective in the justification of the sinner. In this case, faith alone, the *pistis* of St. Paul, already contains everything spiritual, both the love that is alive in good works and the hope that is total reliance on the promises of Christ.

VIII. THOMAS AQUINAS

In the theological method of Thomas Aquinas, Scholasticism turned Catholic hermeneutics around. Indeed, as preacher and as poet the Angelic Doctor was not averse to providing spiritual senses that were familiar to his times. Yet as theologian he was quite clear that "only the literal sense provides demonstrative arguments."[97] In other words, what emerges from spiritual or allegorical interpretations is not the revelation. This is given by the very letter of Scripture. The spiritual senses suggest applications to the circumstances of life as faith inspires charity and hope. Yet the letter itself, *sacra pagina*, "the sacred page," is the norm of faith and thereby of theological judgment. In the structure of the Summa, "authorities," that is, appropriate passages from Scripture or from some of the Fathers of the church, constitute the principle of Thomas's response (introduced by *sed contra*) to the various opinions

---

[97]   *Summa theologiae*, I, q. 1, a. 10, ad 1.

that have just been listed. *Sed contra* determines the moment when the diverse suggestions of theologians and doctors are brought to a stop by the testimony of the written Word. It is in this testimony that Thomas's solution, expounded in the body of his response, finds its starting point and its ultimate justification.

When medieval theologians used formulations that anticipated the Reformers' principle of *Scriptura sola*, they still generally meant Scripture with the spiritual senses that had been expounded in numerous commentaries. Scripture alone, in this case, included its subsequent hermeneutical tradition. But the theological method of Aquinas undoubtedly contributed to downgrading the search for spiritual senses that could be distinct from the literal meaning of Scripture. With Aquinas, the "sacred page," Scripture, designates the literal meaning alone. At the same time, however, Aquinas kept the established scholastic practice of arguing from isolated sentences. The use of pinpointed references to Scripture may have been partly due to the necessity of often working with collections of excerpts rather with full texts. In any case, it also favored an unfortunate collapsing of biblical argumentation into a few words which thereby tended to be given absolute value.

Along with quotations from Scripture the Scholastics argued from quotations from the Fathers of the church, from their own more recent forerunners, and also occasionally from Aristotle and his commentators. But this, in lesser minds, could make Scripture as remote from religious concerns as Aristotle was or, reversely, it could give revelatory value to Aristotle and to what was taken to be the natural law. Such an assumption was not unknown in the theological textbooks of the early twentieth century, when Leo XIII's endorsement of Neo-Scholasticism as the official theology of Catholic seminaries promoted the quasi canonization of what was taken to be the Christian reading of Aristotle.

IX. RECENT QUESTIONS

The place of Scripture in Catholic theology began to change, though slowly, with the spread of modern scientific exegesis. But we have then run into other problems. When the literal sense is no longer identified with what Jesus said and did, but with what various authors, conveying the concerns of whatever local church they knew, interpreted him as saying and doing, the priority of the literal sense needs to be qualified. *Was Christum treibet*, to use Luther's formula, is then far from

evident, unless one can draw on a special insight into the gospel. Such
an insight might come from the previous tradition or from the testimony of the Spirit independently of the present reading of Scripture.
In the absence of a clear criterion for interpreting Scripture and dis-
cerning the Word of God in it, the way is wide open to new kinds of
spiritual senses.

In fact, new meanings need not require drastic revisions of previous principles of interpretation. A small qualification may be enough
to change the whole tone of biblical reading. By drawing attention to
the self-transcendent potentialities of creation, transcendental Thomism
itself opens up not only a new evaluation of the human but also a
sympathetic hearing of the utopian hopes of New Age. Admittedly,
this is not without danger and should not be hailed naively as a break-
through. It calls for critical appraisal. Or let us focus on the preferential
option for the poor, and politics can become a key for interpreting
Scripture, with the unavoidable consequence that conflicting political
readings of Scripture will arise. Bossuet's *Politique tirée de l'Ecriture
Sainte* was cast precisely in that mold, and what he found in Scripture
was a justification of Louis XIV's absolute monarchy. In the eighteenth
century the frequent appeal of pious theologians to divine providence
to explain the existence of poverty and the poor was in the same vein.
The double language of a preferential option for the poor and of spend-
ing millions of dollars on papal journeys is not exempt from the
ambiguity of politics based upon the Scriptures. And whatever their
contemporary justification, the insights and also the problems of liberation theology cannot be totally separated from a similar ambiguity.
Or let us choose an existential key. If this is that of Bultmann, one
obtains a demythologized and in fact soon disincarnate reading of Scripture. But let it be the new awareness of feminine existence, and
hermeneutics is handed another key that opens new insights into the
implications of the gospel. Or let us find a hermeneutical key in
humanity's general search for the Ultimate, and the Jewish and Christian Scriptures become one of many sets in a universal collection of
revelatory texts.

Thus our times are witnessing a new incarnation of the old search
for spiritual meanings in the same texts that have been read, in different
ways, from the beginning. But this search has now been freed from the
classical concern for the theological virtues of faith, love, and hope,
which, all of them being centered in Christ, served to control the old

spiritual exegesis. At this point in the history of biblical reading, however, the patristic-medieval concern for active faith, and the christocentric and soteriological principle of Martin Luther's exegesis, are both in danger of being stifled precisely by new keys to the Scripture.

X. LESSONS OF MODERN LINGUISTICS

It seems to me difficult to speak of reading the Word today without listening to the modern sciences of language. When one speaks of the Word of God in a Christian context, one affirms the existence of a body of writings in which contemporary Christians believe that they have found the Word of God. But this is not only to say that successive communications from God were written down in biblical times and in the century that followed the death of Jesus of Nazareth, or that the history of divine communications to a chosen people can be reconstructed with the help of the Old and the New Testament writings. Given the theology of the Trinity, it is also saying that Scripture is both the Word of God written and also one mode of the presence on earth, among humans, of the eternal Word of God. The eternal Word is also called the eternal Son, the Second Person, the Lord, the Redeemer and Savior, the Wisdom, Image or Icon of God. In relation to him God is called Father, the Unoriginated, the First Person. And his Spirit, the Third Person, spoke through the prophets and now, as Paraclete and Comforter, abides in the Church and in the faithful soul.

A special relationship is thus suggested between Scripture as Word of God and the divine Trinitarian life. Scripture has recorded the word spoken to the prophets and through the evangelists and epistle writers of the New Testament. But there is more to it. It also embodies the presence of the divine Word that no created mind and mouth can speak, and that may be discerned only through faith in an experience that is similar to what Jean Calvin designated as the interior testimony of the Holy Spirit. According to the Christian faith, it is this divine Word who was incarnate as the prophet Jesus of Nazareth, becoming one of us, being seen, heard, and touched, and leaving a memorial of his presence in the eucharistic meal. Scripture is thus profoundly christocentric, focused forward, in the Old Testament and, as it were, backward, in the New, on the events of the birth, life, and death of Jesus, and on the renewed experience of his presence which the disciples called his rising from the dead.

When we speak of the Second Person as Word, we of course speak
analogically. We move in the area of semiotics and symbolism. We
affirm in God that which allows us to use comparisons from human
language and experience to point to God. And as, in human language,
writing is the sign of speech and speech the sign and instrument of
thought, so Scripture is the sign of prophetic words spoken on earth,
which are themselves the sign and instrument of God's eternal Word.
Between Scripture and the eternal Word there is a semiotic relationship. The ultimate meaning of Scripture is the eternal Word as it "became
flesh for us and for our salvation."

XI. THE ULTIMATE MEANING

We are thus faced with the paradox that the ultimate meaning of
Scripture is, in final analysis, ineffable. It lies beyond any attempt at
formulation, whether in a theology of glory or in a theology of the
Cross. "Theologians of glory" have claimed glowing success for their
investigations of God and the divine revelation. More humbly before
the mystery of the death of Christ, "theologians of the Cross," as Luther
perceived, have contemplated the infinite condescension of God who
in the death of Christ proclaims sinners just. Yet in both cases the
reality of God remains hidden—*Deus absconditus*—beyond what is said
and imagined, and no less beyond the human face of Jesus, living, dying, or rising, than beyond the hoped for glory of human achievements.
Thus there always remains a principle of uncertainty in our reading of
Scripture. One may find in this the reason why each coming Christian
generation cannot simply take the Scriptures and the Word of God for
granted but has to receive them anew. This is why the tone and concerns of scientific exegesis vary every five to ten years, why each culture
where the Christian faith has taken hold has come up with new approaches to theology, why in the Roman Empire and in later Europe
Eastern and Western insights have differed, and why at the present
time Africa, Asia, and Latin America are opening new avenues to the
Scriptures, as are likewise doing some sections of Christian society for
which Scripture was, until recently, a relatively closed book. No human culture and no sum total of human cultures can adequately grasp
the meaning of Scripture as the imprint of the eternal Word.

One may be tempted to conclude from this to a reverent agnosti-
cism regarding the possibility of formulating the meaning of Scripture
in human language. And this could open up the gate to a manifold

exploitation of Scripture by partisan concerns. For if, the ultimate
meaning being ineffable, there is no recognizable standard of interpretation, then there would seem to be no checks and balances on misuses
of the text. The proper control, however, is already available in the
fundamental principle that Scripture is not given in order to be used.
Scripture is used when we place ourselves above the text in order to
determine its meaning. When one realizes that the only possible place
for the Church, its members, and its officers is below the Word, in a
stance of expectancy, of attention, of listening, then the text itself acquires its correct dimension. It becomes a medium for obedient
encounter with the Word. One may then rightly look for a canon within
the canon, for a sign, within the semiotic system or systems of Scripture, that the Word is present. Luther's search for *was Christum treibet*
constitutes historically the first major attempt to discern such a norm.
Yet even this does not solve the problem of the meaning of Scripture.

To say that Scripture is a writing, a text, a discourse is to imply
that, whatever its ultimate meaning as Word of God, it falls within the
structures of human language. If God communicates with us through
prophets and apostles, then God has no choice but to speak a human
language. A text depends originally on the intention of its author and
eventually on that of its redactor or redactors. Yet, like a work of art, it
soon acquires a life of its own, independently of the author's intent.
The language used follows its own laws, of which the writers may well
have been unaware, but which are no less effectively at work for their
unawareness. The language follows not only the laws of its formulation at the moment when it is spoken, but also the laws of its reception
at the moment when it is heard or read. Like all language, then, Scripture becomes a syntagma that may be analyzed and formalized. It lies
open to the test of paradigmatic commutation. Above all, it develops
the mythical dimension that is to be found in all writing about the
absolute and the transcendent. Scripture becomes the written myth of
Christianity, which may be systematically compared with other myths
of humankind, even though, in the experience of the faithful it belongs
to a level that is not reached by other myths, the level of the eternal
Word, and to an event that shatters the numinous content of all myths,
the event of the Cross of Jesus.

Hugh's pattern of letter, sense, and *sententia* can now be reinterpreted. At the moment of letter, research leads the reader into the
semiotics of scriptural discourse. At the moment of sense, several levels

of significance are unveiled in the discourse. As to the moment of *sententia*, it is a presumably rare ineffable instant when the reader is lifted above the letter and its immediate meaning into the realm of the Spirit. Carried by God's love from grace to grace, one may then, like St. Paul, "hear ineffable words that it is not permitted to man to repeat" (2 Cor 12:4). In such words the ultimate meaning of Scripture is reached: it is identical with the eternal Word.

XII. THE ECUMENICAL TASK

In all of today's churches, I am afraid, the actual and even the official resonance of Scripture falls short of what it should be. We are not yet far removed from the conception of Scripture as words dictated by God, which convey the divine revelation in propositional form. At the same time the churches have not effectively renounced the notion that Scripture is at the disposal of ministers as a quarry of quotable matter. Proof texts or illustrations are extracted regardless of their sense in context. If they cannot be taken literally, then one can still rely on allegory to make a point, yet without the sophisticated understanding of allegory that was familiar to our medieval ancestors. Even papal documents and the decrees of Vatican II mine Scripture for illustration of themes rather than as the one source and norm of the language of faith. Between the fundamentalist and the liberal wings of Christian thought, most theologians refer to Scripture as from the outside, according to the speculative concerns and needs of the moment.

This, then, points to the remaining ecumenical task. Vatican II declared: "Like the Christian religion itself, all church proclamation must feed on, and be ruled by, Holy Scripture. The Word of God contains such force and efficacy that it stands out for the Church as nourishment and health and for the Church's children as strength of their faith, food for their soul, pure and perennial font of their spiritual life" (*Dei Verbum*, no. 21). And again: "...the study of the sacred text should be, so to speak, the soul of sacred theology" (no. 24). The task ahead for the churches that desire reconciliation is to find their common soul. The process can be put simply, in words of admonition that are addressed to a new bishop in the contemporary Roman ritual for the ordination of a bishop: "Believe what you read, practice what you believe, preach what you practice."

This point should throw light on the internal and the external dialogue of the churches. In their internal dialogue within their common profession of the Christian faith, it is my opinion that the first phase of ecumenical conversations is now over. The doctrines over which Catholics and Protestants have differed historically have been abundantly debated. And a series of agreed statements have considerably narrowed the field of divergence. The official dialogues have succeeded in reducing the differences to a minimum which, I should think, hardly justifies the continuing separation of the churches at the level of faith. These agreements of course still need to be received and assimilated. But this will be chiefly a matter of time. In the meanwhile one has to start thinking about opening the second phase. Christians now need to dialogue about their use, misuse, and abuse of the Scriptures, which were not meant, in the first place, to be used. They should together—not separately—learn how not to be "above God's word," and how to serve "the Word, teaching only what has been transmitted..." (*Dei Verbum*, no. 10). This dialogue should begin with a fundamental reexamination of principles and practices in trying to listen to the Word of God and to draw from this the proper conclusions regarding practical Christian living. We have a long way to go before this second phase can be satisfactorily implemented.

XIII. THE CATECHISM OF THE CATHOLIC CHURCH

This sense of an unfinished task has been heightened for me by reading the *Catechism of the Catholic Church* as issued in French at the end of 1992. Parallel to the *Catechismus romanus* or "Catechism of the Council of Trent," which embodied the Tridentine teachings, this volume purports to embody the teachings of Vatican II in a simple form that may serve as a model for the teaching of catechism. It follows the general plan of the Catechism of the Council of Trent, as it draws attention, possibly borrowing the language of Islam, to "four pillars," namely, the creed or profession of faith, the sacraments of faith, the commandments or life of faith, and the Lord's Prayer or prayer of the believer. The text is made of quotations from the Council with occasional additions and comments.

Starting from the assertion that "man is *capax Dei*" by creation,[98] the First Part explains that God revealed himself from the beginning, and then through Noah, Abraham, the people of Israel, and finally through "Christ Jesus, the Mediator and the Fullness of all the Revela-

---

[98]   *Catéchisme*, sect. I, ch. 1, p. 21.

tion."[99] This revelation has been "transmitted" by the "apostolic tradition" which is made of "the apostolic preaching" and "apostolic succession." As written down after "the first generation of Christians," the Scripture of the New Testament "testifies to the process of the living Tradition."[100]

This approach, however, does not lead the catechism to consider the variety of and the dynamic exchanges within the living tradition that emerge from the christological diversity of the New Testament. Nor does it lead, as it could conceivably do, to an Augustinian analysis of self-knowledge in the light of God-knowledge, as at the beginning of Calvin's Institutes. In a typical move in the spirit of the Counter Reformation, it leads to the remarkable feat of affirming "the magisterium of the Church," immediately identified as "the bishops in communion with the successor of Peter, the bishop of Rome,"[101] even before any consideration of the Word of God in Scripture and in the early tradition before the episcopal hierarchy had become effective.

The more detailed article on Holy Scripture comes last in a three-pronged presentation of "God encountering Man" (ch. 2), that is, in revelation (art. I), in the transmission of revelation (art. 2), in the Holy Scripture (art. 3). This article is a very brief summary of the constitution *Dei Verbum* (five paragraphs: Christ as the one Word of Scripture, inspiration and truth of Scripture, the Holy Spirit as interpreter of Scripture, the canon of the Scriptures, Scripture in the church's life). The commentary insists on "the intention of the sacred authors," but it makes no allusion to contemporary debates on hermeneutics; and it includes a section on the four senses of Scripture and their "profound concordance."[102]

This, in my judgment, does justice neither to the present wealth of biblical studies in Catholic circles, nor to the findings of the theology of tradition that preceded and followed Vatican II, and still less to the richness of the Catholic reflection on Scripture and its tradition that was nurtured by those developments.

---

[99]   *Catéchisme*, p. 28.

[100] *Catéchisme*, ch. 2, p. 32.

[101] *Catéchisme*, p. 32.

[102] *Catéchisme*, p. 37.

XIV. THE EXTERNAL DIALOGUE

Still another perspective can be opened, even if it is difficult to look far down into it. As was suggested above in relation to the available hermeneutical keys that lie around the present theological workshop, the ecumenical horizon has been considerably broadened in recent years in the context of what was called for some time "the wider ecumenism" and is now called "the encounter of religions" or the "dialogue between religions." This undoubtedly raises new questions for the Christian doctrine of the Word of God. There is also, or there should be, next to the internal dialogue of Christians about the Word of God, an external dialogue. The church's external dialogue is this beginning encounter between all the great religions of the world. Without passing judgment on the intrinsic values of the world religions as ways of knowing and loving God, and even while holding that there can only be idolatry outside of the divine grace and revelation given in Christ, one may see the religions as cultural developments that have specified particular ways of being human.

Whatever one prefers to name this movement, it is clear that many religions outside the biblical stream recognize some Scriptures as somehow divine revelation. Indeed, the Christian inquiry into the meaning of Scripture points to the need of understanding the place of sacred writings in the other religions that claim to have some. One may then wonder how a Christian may read the Scriptures that have developed outside the Judeo-Christian stream.

Indeed one may view the Koran as a lengthy meditation on the Creator, that is precisely focused on the central affirmation of the greatness and sovereignty of the Creator. Moreover, the ninety-nine "beautiful names" of God—the names that are found in the Koran—invite Christian believers to further reflection on the divine attributes. There are also the sacred writings of the monotheistic religions, old as in Zoroastrianism (the Gâthas and other texts of the Avesta), or more recently like the sacred writings of the Sikhs. And one may add the quasi-scriptural status of the Talmud or of the Kabbalah in some forms of later Judaism. And what of those writings that have come to function as additional to the Bible in many heterodox movements that have grown out of Christianity?

There are further problems in relation to the meaning of Scriptures outside of the monotheistic religions in the strict sense. What can it mean that some writings are recognized as sacred when there is no

belief in one absolute Creator who speaks through them or has inspired them? There are the Vedas, the Upanishads and the great epics
of Hinduism, that include the Bhagavad Gîta. There is the Tripitaka of
Buddhism in both the Small and the Great Vehicles. What does it mean
for Hindus to have Sacred Writings, when orthodox Hinduism is divided in six darçanas, or schools of thought, some of which appear to
have little in common? What does it say about the Christian conception of Scripture as divine Word that the Triple Basket of the Buddhist
Scriptures has become so huge and contains so many writings that it is
quite impossible to read them all?

Even apart from their experiences of holy scriptures, Hinduism
and Buddhism raise questions that cannot be eluded indefinitely. Vedânta
challenges Christianity in regard to the divine attribute of eternity and
its relevance to the transcendence and the immanence of God. Buddhism challenges Christian theology in regard to the apophatic
knowledge of the transcendent that is touched upon but hardly developed in classical Scholasticism. Such questions are growing at the
ecumenical horizon.

XV. CONCLUSION

There are now some discouraged ecumenists. They are generally
waiting for church authorities and agencies to commit the churches to
action on the basis of the findings of official and other commissions.
And they are tempted to give up the hope that promises, brilliant as
they were at one time, will be followed by action. When it started in
the early years of our finishing century, the ecumenical movement was
intended to move the churches and the Church. But it does not seem to
have moved much more than itself. Yet if there is a lesson to learn from
the present stagnant state of relations among Christian churches and
their leaders, it is not that hope can be given up. It is that, whatever
convictions they have correctly reached, the bilateral and other commissions of dialogue have not made a persuasive case for those who
have not taken part in their dialogues and read their agreed or joint
statements with the critical eyes of outsiders. Indeed "the harvest is
ready" but the churches at large are not quite ready for it. The tools
need further sharpening. There is still a great deal of work to do.

LIST OF CONTRIBUTORS

Rev. Dr. Joseph A. Burgess
Director
Institute for Lutheran Historical Studies
Regent Lutheran Parish
Regent, ND

Professor Kenneth Hagen
Department of Theology
Marquette University
Milwaukee, WI

Rev. Daniel J. Harrington, S.J.
Weston School of Theology
Cambridge, MA

Professor Grant R. Osborne
Trinity Evangelical Divinity School
Deerfield, IL

Rev. Dr. Michael Prokurat
Adjunct Faculty
Pacific Lutheran Theological Seminary
Berkeley, CA
St. Nicholas Orthodox Church
San Anselmo, CA

Rev. George H. Tavard, A.A.
Distinguished Professor
Presidential Chair in Theology
Marquette University
Milwaukee, WI